Under the Jumper

Under the Jumper

Autobiographical Excursions

GYLES BRANDRETH

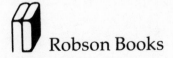

Robson Books

First published in Great Britain in 1993 by Robson Books Ltd, Bolsover House, 5–6 Clipstone Street, London W1P 7EB

British Library Cataloguing in Publication Data
A catalogue record for this book is available from the British Library

ISBN 0 86051 894 9

Photoset in North Wales by Derek Doyle and Associates, Mold, Clwyd.

Printed in Great Britain by Butler & Tanner Ltd, Frome and London.

CONTENTS

Acknowledgements

As this book takes the form of a letter to my son, I had planned to call it *Dear Boy*. Given my past association with colourful knitwear, my publisher felt that *Under the Jumper* would be more commercial. I hope he is right, but I have my doubts. The Librarian at the House of Commons misread the catalogue and sent me a note expressing the hope that I might present a copy of my new book to the Library. She called it *Under the Juniper...* Now that's a book I'd like to write. Perhaps one day, I will. Meanwhile, I would like to thank my family for allowing me to use my summer holiday to write this. My thanks also to Jenny Noll for typing the manuscript and to her sister, Liz Noll, for checking it. Thanks too to David Rarrell, Bill Potter, Philip Ingram, Francis Loney, Michael Gell, Sidney Harris, the *Birmingham Post*, the *Daily Mail*, TV-am, Yorkshire TV, Keystone Press, for permission to reproduce their photographs.

AMBITION

'I must keep aiming higher and higher – even though I know how
silly it is.'

Aristotle Onassis

On my desk I have a card sent to me by the Reverend
Clifford Warren, Rector of Machen, a Welsh clergyman
who, when I appeared regularly on television, was in the
habit of sending in telling maxims and homespun homilies
for me to share with the viewing millions. On this card he has
written: 'Beginning. The word "begin" is full of energy. The
best way to get something done is to *begin*. It's truly
amazing what tasks we can accomplish if only we begin.
You're never finished if you for ever keep beginning.'

So, here I am at the beginning of what is probably the first
letter I have ever sent to you. Because I was away at
boarding school for much of my childhood, my parents
wrote to me regularly, but because you have always lived at
home there has never been a need to write. There isn't a need
now, but before I lose you – and I will lose you, just as my
father lost me – there are one or two things I wanted to tell
you, and a few stories I wanted to share, in the hope that they
might make you smile. We chat a lot, but we don't talk very
often. You have been central to my life now for eighteen
years and here you are, coming of age, and I don't believe we
have had one long, leisurely, *profound* conversation.

Candidly, I doubt you'll find anything especially profound in the pages that follow, but you can regard this as edited highlights of the ramblings you might have got had I been one of those fathers who stands with his back to the fire and offers his son worldly advice marinaded in gentle reminiscence.

Mary Soames told me how her father, Sir Winston Churchill, when he was an old man, would sit at the head of the dinner table at Chartwell and tell his family stories late into the night. When the candles began to gutter and Lady Churchill would suggest that perhaps it was time for bed, Sir Winston would recharge the brandy glass, raise his hand as if to halt an imaginary clock from striking and instruct his wife: 'Command the moment to remain.'

You will find a number of prime ministers in the pages that follow, but precious few Churchillian flourishes. I am enormously ambitious for you and I hope you will be ambitious for yourself. I'd be delighted for you to be Prime Minister some day (and, remember, somebody's got to be Prime Minister so, if you're interested, it might as well be you), but I am content for you to set your own goals. Like every father, my ambition is for you to be happy and to fulfil your potential. Of course, happiness and self-fulfilment don't happen by chance. They need to be achieved.

I subscribe to the 'hierachy of motives' developed by the psychologist Abraham Maslow in the 1950s. Maslow devised a pyramid of human needs, ascending from the fundamental biological needs present at birth to the more complex psychological needs that become important only after the more basic needs have been satisfied:

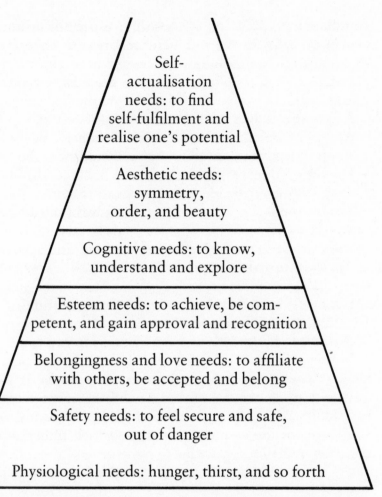

Self-
actualisation
needs: to find
self-fulfilment and
realise one's potential

Aesthetic needs:
symmetry,
order, and beauty

Cognitive needs: to know,
understand and explore

Esteem needs: to achieve, be competent, and gain approval and recognition

Belongingness and love needs: to affiliate
with others, be accepted and belong

Safety needs: to feel secure and safe,
out of danger

Physiological needs: hunger, thirst, and so forth

Do you remember the moment in *The Graduate* where the businessman by the pool offers Dustin Hoffman the ultimate in life-advice: 'I have just one word to say to you, young man: plastics!' Well, it seems I have just one word, albeit hyphenated, to offer you: 'Self-actualisation'. As a word, it lacks poetry. As a concept, it is worth exploring. To build a composite picture of the true self-actualiser Maslow studied the lives of a group of remarkable individuals who, without argument, could be said to have made extraordinary use of their potential – Spinoza, Einstein, Thomas Jefferson,

Abraham Lincoln, Eleanor Roosevelt, and the like – and then developed a list of the specific characteristics they share. It seems true self-actualisers:

Perceive reality efficiently and are able to tolerate uncertainty;

Accept themselves and others for what they are;

Are spontaneous in thought and behaviour;

Are problem-centred rather than self-centred;

Have a good sense of humour;

Are highly creative;

Are resistant to enculturation, although not purposely unconventional;

Are concerned for the welfare of humanity;

Are capable of deep appreciation of the basic experiences of life;

Establish deep, satisfying interpersonal relations with a few, rather than many, people;

Are able to look at life from an objective viewpoint.

Knowing you as I do, my boy, I think you're in with a chance! And to help you on your way, Maslow also produced a list of aspects of behaviour that will help lead you towards self-fulfilment and the realisation of your potential:

Experience life as a child does, with full absorption and concentration;

Try something new rather than sticking to secure and safe ways;

Listen to your own feelings in evaluating experiences rather than to the voice of tradition or authority or the majority (if you do go into politics, you'll find the Whips sometimes make this one a little tricky);

Be honest, avoid pretences or 'game playing';

Be prepared to be unpopular if your views don't coincide with those of most people;

Assume responsibility;

Try to identify your defences and have the courage to give them up;

Work hard at whatever you decide to do.

And if you can decide *what* you want to do that's a good start. The enviable people are those who know at twenty where they are going and what they want to do. In worldly terms, the secret of success is to have a goal and to go for it. If you know you want to be a barrister or a ballet dancer (I think the former rather than the latter in your case) the more blessed is your state. You won't hit a target unless you have one. Whatever it is, start at the bottom, don't be deceived by short-cuts (there aren't any), don't be distracted by diversions (they are usually cul-de-sacs), and the chances are you'll get where you want in the end – or way before it.

According to the yellowing cutting that sits before me, when I was twenty I told the *Sun* that my ambition was to be 'A sort of Danny Kaye and then Home Secretary'. The reason that the *Sun*, in its pre-tabloid incarnation, had sought me out was that in 1968 I was briefly regarded as an 'Oxford personality', not as celebrated as Beverley Nichols had been immediately after the First World War, nor as notorious as Kenneth Tynan had become after the Second, but none the less a 'university character' in the same tradition, not a figure of any substance or significance, but one that Fleet Street (as it then was) would light on and feature. Some stories are predictable: every other year a minister resigns to spend more time with his family, it rains during Wimbledon fortnight, a broadsheet features a photograph of a duck and her brood crossing a main road, Noddy and Billy Bunter are attacked by a librarian, and a student (more often than not, an Oxbridge undergraduate) is written up rather more than he or she deserves. I was written up extensively.

In his day at Oxford, Beverley Nichols was written up even more extensively. Since you have not heard of him (though you will find his first autobiography, written when he was twenty-five, in my study) you will be amazed to learn that he wasn't just well-known: he was famous. A *wunderkind* of the roaring twenties, he was a prolific writer of waspish charm who became best known eventually for his prowess with a trowel and his fondness for cats. (I believe the *Beverley Nichols Cats' Calendar* still finds an audience each Christmas.) Mr Nichols' term as President of the Union at Oxford occurred exactly half a century before mine, so I held an anniversary debate in his honour. My reward was a delightful lunch (cheese soufflé, cucumber salad, chilled Sancerre) with the great man and his boyfriend at Sudbrook Cottage, their house on Ham Common, where my host proudly showed off his resplendent garden and his latest book of flower-arranging, in which his masterstroke was a striking arrangement featuring a whole red cabbage as the centrepiece. He could do extraordinary things with flowers including, on the occasion of a visit by a ladies' gardening circle, the placing of an exquisite arrangement of miniature roses in the lavatory bowl in the downstairs loo. When the green-fingered ladies, refreshed with a cup or two of Beverley's excellent Lapsang, went out to relieve themselves each was confronted with a truly disconcerting dilemma.

Kenneth Tynan could be deliberately disconcerting too. A better writer than Beverley Nichols (and a better theatre critic than almost anybody), he is remembered as the man who pioneered nudity on stage with *O Calcutta!* and first said 'fuck' on television. This is a pity because his writing has stood the test of time (for the most readable portrait of British theatre in the fifties and early sixties read Tynan's *Curtains*) and he was a key member of the team when Olivier was establishing the National Theatre. (Tip for you if you decide to go into the theatre: read plays, old plays, new plays, obscure plays, hits of yesteryear, the lot. Actors don't read plays. Ask almost any actor what part he'd most like to play, and he's either stumped or falls back on a predictable standby. Actors are often infuriated by presumptuous directors with intellectual pretensions (especially when they are young), but in the theatre – as in other spheres – a readiness to read can give you the upper hand.)

Tynan was more gifted, more complex, but less secure, less contented than Nichols. Even at twenty I could tell that an emaciated middle-aged man who offered a girl a fiver to take off her jumper for him had problems. In fairness, the offer was made in the interests of art (well, television) as much as personal gratification. The BBC brought Tynan and a documentary film crew to Oxford and, since these were the Swinging Sixties, and the BBC was shooting an under-graduate party on a boat on the Isis, a topless reveller was clearly essential. In the event, the director lost his nerve, Tynan kept his fiver, the girl kept her modesty and, by way of alternative, I was persuaded to jump into the river crying 'Whoopee!'. (You may have seen this clip on *Newsnight* at the time of Bill Clinton's election. The BBC revived it to give a flavour of the 42nd President's student days.) Altogether I spent quite a time in the Isis for Tynan in the summer of 68. Another sequence in the documentary centred on my apparent search for the most beautiful girl in Oxford, the Zuleika Dobson of her day. A dozen young lovelies were gathered in ball gowns on the banks of the river and, in homage to Max Beerbohm's story, I proceeded to march resolutely into the river when confronted with the unattainable beauty of the loveliest of them. (On the director's advice my Zuleika Dobson was Lady Annunziata Asquith, not because her profile was the prettiest but because it was the highest.)

What propelled me to make myself an 'Oxford figure' was an unspoken feeling that my father expected it. All I knew of Oxford when I went up in 1967 was what my father had told me of his time there forty years before. This may have been the sixties of student revolt, protest marches, permissible pot and sexual liberation, but I rolled into the city of dreaming spires with the aspirations (and, I fear, something of the manner) of a young man of the 1920s. From within the time capsule I was inhabiting, the trio to pull off was conquering the Union, editing the *Isis* and directing the OUDS.

Becoming President of the Union I managed with a series of fruity oratorical displays of the old school – and not too many of them: enough to impress, but not so many as to let the novelty wear off or the mechanics become too obvious. I planted my foot on the first rung of the *Isis* ladder in my first term by offering the magazine an irresistibly shocking (so I thought and so it proved) piece entitled 'The Breast'. I climbed the ladder by dint of persistence and application. I have found, as a rule, that it's the only way.

BEAUTY

'Beauty is a good letter of introduction.'
German Proverb

Jane Asher was the first undeniably beautiful woman to sleep in my bed. Maddeningly, I was elsewhere at the time.

We are all in agreement, of course, that it's what happens between the ears, rather than between the sheets, that counts, but I have to tell you that in the summer of 1968, Jane, with her pallor, her fragility, her sumptuous red hair, her wide eyes, was quite inordinately fanciable.

I had seen her on screen in *The Greengage Summer* and *Alfie*; I had seen her on stage in Edinburgh in *The Winter's Tale* and in Toronto in *Measure for Measure*; I had thought of her often and, at this distance in time I think I can admit it, I had thought of her longingly in an uncomplicated way; and now here, uninvited, unexpected, but, heaven knows, not unwelcome, she was standing at the door to my room and *asking* to come in and lie down.

This was the end of my first year at Oxford and it was the night of the New College Ball. Jane was around because she was rehearsing at the Playhouse and the director of the piece was giving her a night off and a night out amid the partying undergraduates. It was early evening. The ball didn't kick off till ten. Jane needed somewhere to change and rest and someone suggested that my room in the garden quadrangle was well placed. She came, she slept, she changed, she danced, she went. When I hit it a few hours later my pillow felt different, and better.

(Be warned, my boy, that meeting one's screen goddess isn't always destined to be an unqualified success. Until the age of twelve, Hayley Mills filled my life with meaning and sunshine. A quarter of a century later we had a rather stilted lunch and talked about God, meditation and the meaning of life. I felt distinctly middle-aged.)

Oxford in the late sixties was a good place for meeting beautiful women. When I was President of the Union I invited a young disc jockey turned TV chat show host called Simon Dee to come and debate the nature of pop culture. He rolled up (and if it wasn't in a Rolls, it was in something equally flash but lower, sleeker and faster) with Joanna Lumley on his arm. Simon had everything, talent, looks, flair, charm, a quick way with words and women, but somehow it all went wrong, and at spectacular speed. I still see him daily because he gave me a double-sided coat hanger featuring his head and shoulders, life size, and signed Simon Dee on one side and with his real name, Nicholas Henty-Dodd, on the other, and I always think of him with gratitude and affection because he introduced me to Joanna, who, then as now, exemplified the truth of Christian Dior's observation that zest is the secret of all beauty, 'There is no beauty that is attractive without zest.' (Is that a universal truth? Yes, certainly with Joanna it is her energy, verve, enthusiasm, intelligence that make her glow. Watch her performance and a lot happens. With Jane, it's different. There's stillness, there's strength, there's transparency, but there isn't zest in an obvious way. She appears straightforward and straightforward people can be the most difficult to understand.)

The most celebrated undergraduate actress at Oxford in my time was Diana Quick, best known now, I suppose, for playing Julia Flyte in *Brideshead Revisited* and for living

with Albert Finney and Bill Nighy (consecutively, of course).
(It must be as irritating to be known by the company you've
kept as by the knitwear you've worn. When I had introduced
Jane Asher to Prince Philip at a charity lunch marking his
seventieth birthday he said, 'Didn't she go out with Paul
McCartney?' I said, 'Yes, but that was twenty-five years ago
and I don't think she likes to be reminded of it.' 'Pity,' said
Prince Philip, 'McCartney's a very good chap.') At Oxford in
1968 Diana Quick was a force to reckon with, not because
she was beautiful and brilliant (and she was both) but
because she was President of OUDS.

Like any self-respecting student organisation, the university dramatic society took itself seriously and, as someone
who, in this instance, had broken his own rule and not
worked his way up through the ranks but was attempting to
come in at the top as a comparative outsider, I felt my only
hope was to be a little bit *different*. I might feel I had a right
to direct an OUDS production at the Playhouse as a kind of
paternal gift, but I understood that others might not see it
quite my way. My tactic, therefore, was to offer something
unexpected and irresistible: a traditional English pantomime.

I sent Diana a note introducing myself and enquiring if she
had ever seen herself as a potential Cinderella. She replied by
return, suggesting we meet for a drink. This may have been
the Swinging Sixties, but mine was the spirit of the more
timid twenties and (laugh if you will) to go along to have a
drink with a celebrated but unknown older woman seemed
rather a fast thing to be doing. My sense of danger in her
sophisticated company was compounded by the fact that,
when we met, she was dressed from neck to ankle in black
leather. (Was it black leather? Or was it shiny black plastic?
Either way it had a disturbing, if not altogether unpleasant,
effect on me.)

Even at nineteen I knew that if you don't ask you won't
get, but if you do you might. Clutching my warm tomato
juice, I put in my request and was dismayed to discover that

the production was not, in fact, in her sole gift. I would need to take part in a competitive audition. I did. I appeared before the serried ranks of OUDS officers and assorted hangers-on and held forth. I explained to them, truthfully, that I had just returned from a day trip to Paris (I did not tell them that I had gone there to secure an exclusive interview with the Aga Khan for *Isis*) and I began my presentation with an eye-witness account of the turbulence at the Sorbonne, going on to suggest that with student protests, rioting and unrest around the globe, what Oxford needed right now was not more of the same, but something different, *viz* a pantomime. To give academic credibility to my thesis I quoted the American critic Eric Bentley's maxim: 'When we get up tomorrow morning we may well be able to do without our tragic awareness for an hour or two, but we shall desperately need our sense of the comic.'

As well as giving them the intellectual justification for your proposed production, the members of the auditioning committee expected to see you in action, doing a bit of no-nonsense directing. I rehearsed Diana in a brief love scene – it was a bit of Shakespeare that they set – and my finest moment came when I explained to her that what I wanted her to do to convey the full anguish of her love was to place her top teeth over her bottom lip and close her eyes. Undoubtedly it was at that moment that the OUDS Committee thought, 'Yes, for pantomime, this is our man.'

Cinderella changed my life. Diana had to finish her thesis and couldn't play the title role, so open auditions were held. Over a series of long summer afternoons a stream of young women flowed into the cloisters of New College where they found me, sitting in a canvas-backed director's chair, and Michael Coveney (now theatre critic of the *Observer* but then my choreographer) waiting to put them through their paces. We asked them to read a bit, sing a bit, dance a bit and then to all but one of them I said, 'Thank you, we'll let you know.' To the lone exception I said, 'Would you mind hanging on till the end of the audition?' She waited patiently, watching the afternoon's remaining batch of aspiring Cinders come and go and then, as soon as we were alone, I offered her a part in the chorus and a Chinese meal.

She accepted the Won Ton soup and the special fried rice (half-a-crown for Menu A) but told me what I could do with the part in the chorus. She went off to appear in a college production of *Twelfth Night*. She was never chorus material. She was a sensational Viola and because, having clapped eyes on her I was not going to let her go, I bullied my way into the same company and gave an unseaworthy Sea Captain. I had eyes for the leading lady, but not for my lines. Somewhere I still have the shirt with scrawled on the cuff: 'This is Illyria, lady ...'

So that, my boy, is how I met Michèle, my wife, your mother. It must be said that if you want a legitimate opportunity to take a close look at the loveliest young women of your generation, organising a widely advertised open audition specifically inviting talented and beautiful people to come along seems as good a way as any to set about it.

I like having a beautiful wife because it means that when we've run out of things to say at least I've got something pleasant to look at. That said, don't be fooled by appearances. As someone (I can't remember who) pointed out to me when I was about your age, 'Never forget that the most beautiful girl in the room may have a boil on her bottom and a vacuum in her head.' Of course, it works both ways. As someone else (I remember this time, George Cukor) observed of Vivien Leigh, 'She was often underrated because she was so beautiful.'

While I may have a soft spot for beautiful actresses, it seems that only elderly comics have a penchant for me. As a child in the 1950s, once I had graduated from Muffin the Mule and Mr Turnip, my favourite television programmes were, from the United States, *Circus Boy* and *The Lone*

Ranger, and, from the home grown fare, *Billy Bunter* and *Whack-O!*

Whack-O! was a sit-com set in a minor public school in which 'Professor' Jimmy Edwards starred as the irrascible, blustering headmaster who took to the cane and the bottle with equal ease. When I was in my mid-thirties and in publishing I worked with Jimmy Edwards on his war memoirs (*Six of the Best* by Flight Lieutenant JKO Edwards, DFC) and he invited me down to his house in East Sussex. He met me at the station and drove me to his home at great speed down narrow country lanes and via two pubs. At the first pub, he downed a pint, at the second, two Bloody Marys. Before lunch he opened a bottle of champagne, mixed it with a carton of orange juice, and quaffed the lot from a silver tankard. He grilled us a pair of substantial steaks and we eased ourselves through two good bottles of claret before moving on to handsome balloons of brandy. After lunch, he told me how unhappy he was and suggested we would both find it a cheering experience to take off all our clothes and clamber together into his new hot tub.

Until that moment I hadn't realised that this great bull of a man, with his booming voice and bristling mustaches, was what Barbara Windsor later described to me as 'Tommy Two-ways'. Awash with alcohol, moist-eyed, sprawled like a beached whale on the banquette in his unkempt kitchen, he was a touching sight, but not an enticing one. I declined the hot tub. He snorted and offered me another drink.

Frankie Howerd was not so easily put off. We had enjoyed a not noticeably liquid lunch at Al Gallo d'Oro in Kensington High Street, and after it, rather than go around the corner to his house in Edwardes Square, he suggested we would work more efficiently at his agent's office in Mayfair. As we passed the receptionist, he growled at her, 'This young man and I have a lot of work to do. We do not wish to be disturbed. Is that understood, madam?' The girl gave a little giggle ('Titter ye not') and we proceeded up the stairs and into a spacious panelled room that appeared to be more drawing room than office. Frank gestured towards a leather sofa and, to my surprise, locked the door and pocketed the key. 'We don't want intruders.'

I opened my briefcase and hurriedly pulled out the manuscript we were to work on. 'Yes,' I said nervously, 'there's lots to get through. I told my *wife* I would have a busy afternoon, but I'd be back in time to bath the *children*. I've got three children you know.'

'Never mind that,' said Frank. Then, as he made to sit down beside me on the sofa, his face suddenly contorted, he clutched his thigh and yelped with pain. 'No, no,' he whimpered, his eyes screwed up as though Hattie Jacques were about to plunge in the syringe.

'What is it?'

'It's my groin! No, ooh, ah, ow ...' he grimaced. Continuing to clutch the affected part, Frank slowly pulled himself across the room towards the large partners' desk by the window. He opened a drawer and produced a jar of ointment. 'This is what we need,' he muttered. He then staggered slowly back towards me, thrust the jar of ointment into my hands, undid his belt, pulled down his trousers, lowered his underpants and collapsed in a heap at my side.

He closed his eyes and sighed, 'You know what to do.'

'I don't,' I said hoarsely.

'You do,' he murmured.

'I don't,' I yelped.

'Apply the ointment,' he barked, 'Rub it in.'

'Where?'

He sat up, opened his eyes, exposed himself and said, '*There!*'

'Where?' I gulped.

'There!' he repeated. 'Haven't you seen one before? It's perfectly harmless. Treat it like a muscle!'

Unhappily I couldn't make my excuses and leave because Frank had locked the door and the key was in his right trouser pocket and his trousers were round his ankles on the floor. Instead, I averted my gaze, got to my feet and stood looking out of the window while I waited for him to get dressed and release me from his lair.

My boy, beware of older men bearing ointments. Indeed, beware of older folk altogether. People get to an age when anything that is young is appealing. Sir John Gielgud told me the tale of Sir Herbert Beerbohm-Tree, the turn-of-the-century actor-manager, famous for his Hamlet (described by Max Beerbohm as 'funny without being vulgar') and infamous for his extra-marital dalliances. One night Lady Tree came home to find her husband dining *à deux* with a breathtakingly handsome young actor. She said goodnight, and, as she closed the dining-room door behind her, murmured, 'The port's on the sideboard, Herbert, and, remember, it's adultery just the same.'

As you can tell, I have no tips to offer you on the art of seduction. I am advised that a flat stomach, a neat bottom and impeccable personal cleanliness will make you more appealing. My own observation also suggests that it's probably more important to be funny than to be gorgeous. On second thoughts, that's the line that Woody Allen took and look where it got him.

CHILDHOOD

'Childhood is the country that produces the most nostalgic, contentious and opinionated exiles.'

Richard Eder

Now you are eighteen, I imagine you reckon your childhood is behind you. How has it been? Has it been good? I do hope so. My childhood was glorious. I felt tremendously grown-up throughout it.

I was born in 1948 (in the aftermath of the 1947 fuel crisis) in a British Forces Hospital in Germany. My parents were stationed in Hanover as part of the Allied Control Commission and, apart from holidays, I spent the first four years of my life in Germany. I don't remember a moment of it, which is rather hard on my parents who clearly expended a lot of time and energy (to say nothing of cash) giving me a good time. While youth may be wasted on the young, babyhood seems to be a complete wash-out if you can recollect none of it. The night before last I was staying with Nicky and Sebastian Coe in Cornwall and I dandled their enchanting baby daughter on my knee. She is a perfect eleven month old, who sleeps soundly all night and gurgles delightfully all day. We struck up an excellent relationship, blowing bubbles and kisses at one another at bathtime, and waving our toast fingers at each other over breakfast. Why will the encounter stick in my tired old mind, but make no lasting impression on her fresh young one?

17

At the age of four I could speak English and German and my parents were convinced I had a gift for languages. When we returned to London they couldn't find a German school for me, so decided to extend my range and sent me instead to the French Lycée in South Kensington, where the high watermark of my career was to be my encounter with General Charles de Gaulle, wartime hero and President of France. The year was 1957, I was nine years old and quite small. De Gaulle was older, taller and on a State visit to the United Kingdom that included lunch at Number Ten, dinner at Buckingham Palace and tea in between at the Lycée Français de Londres where a selected band of pupils was to be presented to him. For weeks we were carefully drilled in anticipation of the great day. We memorised all seven verses of the French National Anthem (*oui, mon petit, sept!*) and, time and again, we rehearsed the firm handshake that was to be accompanied by a smart bob of the head.

At long last *le jour de gloire est arrivé* and, at the given hour, I and half a dozen other representatives of Anglo-French youth were lined up outside the Lycée awaiting the arrival of the presidential limousine. Absolutely on schedule, the great man stepped from his car, was greeted reverentially by our headmaster and led towards the line where we boys and girls were waiting. I was fourth to be presented. President de Gaulle shook the hand of the first pupil. Then he shook the hand of the second pupil. Next he shook the hand of the third pupil and even exchanged a few words with her. Then he shook the hand of the fifth pupil. And then the sixth. And then the seventh. And then the eighth. And then he was away, into the building and out of my life.

I knew I was small, but I hadn't felt that small before. Inevitably I consoled myself with the thought that the slight had not been deliberate, that the President was so tall he simply had not noticed the shrimp standing fourth in the line-up. I wouldn't be recounting this story now if ten years

later, when I was at Oxford, I hadn't been invited to have tea
with Harold Macmillan. Knowing that Supermac and de
Gaulle had known each other over half a century, I thought
the anecdote of my failed encounter with the champion of
the free French might amuse the former Prime Minister.
When I arrived at the tea party I discovered Mr Macmillan
was already there, ensconced in an armchair by the fire and
dozing gently. My hosts said it would be a shame to disturb
him. I waited over two hours for the great man to rouse
himself. I enjoyed three toasted tea cakes and several
sandwiches, but sadly no small talk with Harold Macmillan.
He slept throughout our encounter and I slipped away
without even shaking him by the hand. That night I realised
that he and de Gaulle had been in it together.

Mention of sandwiches reminds me that the best part of
my Lycée years was coming home to a tea of Marmite and
tomato sandwiches and a cold glass of chocolate-flavoured
Nesquik. I was happy at the Lycée. I was just as happy when
I was sent off to boarding school and couldn't understand
why the mothers always shed tears on the platform at
Charing Cross and why Barrington Minor, who was in my
dormitory, cried himself to sleep every night for two years.

Like so many English prep schools, Betteshanger was
located in what had been a minor stately home, with pleasing
grounds (in the terraced Dutch gardens I gave my first Feste
in *Twelfth Night* and my last Rosalind in *As You Like It*) and
a wonderfully committed and intermittently eccentric staff. If
I share my most vivid memories with you – particularly of
the matron who was said to wear no knickers, and of the
other matron who ran off with the games master, and of the
choir master who wore lilac suede shoes and offered tuck in
return for a cuddle – I will give the wrong impression. Yes,
there was a flavour of *Vile Bodies*, but it seemed quite
wholesome at the time and the splendid headmaster, who
was eighty, was in no doubt about his priorities. I still have
the postcard he sent me when I left. The message ran to four

words: 'Keep your Latin accurate.'

When I visit schools nowadays, and there are thirty-seven in my constituency, I spend hours touring the classrooms, inspecting the equipment, debating the nature of the curriculum and the validity (or otherwise) of data gathered by testing and sundry other 'performance indicators'. Ensuring that schools are properly resourced and securing the right academic results are fundamental, obviously, but my own recollection of school life revolves entirely around two or three individual teachers and the myriad activities that took place out of school hours. While I favour league tables I am not sure that they would prove a reliable guide to what made Betteshanger worthwhile from my point of view.

At thirteen I went on to Bedales, near Petersfield in Hampshire, a co-educational boarding school that had once been radical and pioneering, but by the time I arrived was becoming merely fashionable. In 1962, the school's founder, John Badley, was alive, well, one hundred, and living in a cottage in the school grounds. On a Wednesday afternoon I took tea with the old boy and we played Scrabble. Mr Badley and I played scores of games during the year or so I knew him and invariably he won. He won, a) because he was the better player; b) because I had to let him use obsolete words since he insisted they had been current in his youth; and c) because his housekeeper kept the score and I rather think she may have cooked the books. (As she also cooked the scones and had trained as a physiotherapist I felt it best not to complain.) None the less, I yearned to beat Mr Badley at least once in my life – and his. I went into serious training, made a determined effort to increase my vocabulary and memorised those useful little words like yex and jo and xi and, just as the great man was entering his one hundred and second year, beat him by four points. A month later he was dead. I have hardly dared win a game of Scrabble since.

Mr Badley had been a friend of Oscar Wilde and he told me that much of Wilde's wit was 'studied'. He recalled staying at a house party in Cambridge with Wilde and travelling back with him to London by train. Assorted fellow guests came to the station to see Wilde and Badley on their way. At the moment the train was due to pull out, Wilde delivered his valedictory *bon mot*, then the guard blew the whistle and waved his green flag, the admirers on the platform cheered, Wilde sank back into his seat and the train moved off. Unfortunately, it only moved a yard or two before juddering to a halt. The group on the platform gathered again outside the compartment occupied by Badley and Wilde. Oscar hid behind his newspaper and hissed to his companion, 'They've had my parting shot. I only prepared one.'

Wilde was just one of the many celebrated folk who sent their offspring to Bedales. It was (and perhaps still is) a school where the parents rather than the children turn out to be the achievers. Distinguished poets seemed to be the mainstay of the PTA in my day. Tamsin Day-Lewis, Tomas Graves and Sappho Durrell were pupils in my time and each managed (unselfconsciously) to maintain a poetic (and vaguely pre-Raphaelite) aura about them. Sappho's life ended in tragedy and even at thirteen there was something 'different' about her. She was beautiful and she was kind. I say that because one summer Sunday evening I gave her a rose, and she said thank you and kept it. At least, she kept it until she disappeared out of sight behind the science block when she may well have chucked it in the dustbin for all I know. There was another gorgeous girl to whom I gave a rose that summer. She was more obviously beautiful than Sappho and a lot less poetic. 'Pooks' was her nickname and when I presented her with my flower she laughed out loud and immediately dropped it in the gutter.

Four or five years ago I found myself booked to speak at a ladies' luncheon club in the West Midlands. When the club secretary telephoned to finalise the details she said, 'You'll meet up with an old school friend when you come.

Apparently, she used to be known as Spooks or Spooky or something and you were quite smitten.'

When my train arrived at Birmingham New Street the club chairman was on hand to greet me and transport me to the lunch in her labrador-scented Volvo. She was a stout farmer's wife with an oppressively ruddy complexion and a small but perceptible lone hair growing out of her chin. I didn't feel nostalgic enquiries about Pooks would be quite her scene, so we talked about the Milk Marketing Board until we reached the hotel. Over lunch we covered the price of potatoes and the folly of set-aside. Throughout my speech I scanned the faces peering up at me in search of Pooks. I couldn't see her, but I wasn't wearing my contact lenses.

Back at New Street, as I clambered out of the Volvo, the stout middle-aged farmer's wife leant across the gear lever and said, 'You don't remember me, do you?' I swear to you, there were tiny tears in the corner of Pooks's pudgy eyes.

I had more success with Chrissie. She wasn't at Bedales, but she had been. She was the sister of a girl in my class and when our relationship began she was eighteen and I was four years her junior. She came back to the school to see a production of *Murder in the Cathedral* in which I had a walk-on part as one of the monks. I hadn't heard of Chrissie and I certainly had no idea she was in the audience until two or three days after the performance when I received a ten page letter from her that began, 'My dearest darling Gyles, I saw you in the play on Friday and I have to tell you that I am now in love. Don't laugh. This is real. This is true. This is beautiful.' This is odd, I thought, but not unpleasant. She enclosed a photograph, taken in a nightclub in Beirut (this was 1962 remember), and an invitation to me to write back and share my hopes and dreams and 'innermost, *innermost*, INNERMOST' thoughts with her. I wrote back. I have no idea what I said, but I have kept each and every one of the hundred and more increasingly intimate letters she sent to me over the next two years.

One day, when I was sixteen, I was lying on my bed in my dormitory reading Hilary Spurgeon's tome on Shakespeare's imagery, when a boy (who happens now to be Principal Private Secretary to the Chancellor of the Duchy of Lancaster) came in and said, 'Your friend Chrissie is in the quad. She wants to see you.'

Chrissie and I had never met. I didn't want to meet her now. I waited. Another message came. I got up, combed my hair, and went down into the quadrangle. I recognised her at once. She looked even more lustrous than her photograph. She didn't recognise me at all. Within three minutes we had worked out that the boy she had wanted to correspond with had been another of the monks in *Murder in the Cathedral*. Chrissie's sister had identified me by mistake. I never heard from her again.

Losing Chrissie was a relief really. I missed her letters, but I was glad to be spared the necessity of writing back. I had so much else to do. At school I was always busy-busy-busy, editing the school magazine, organising the cycling proficiency tests, playing at politics (I was the Tory candidate, I imagine self-selected, in the school's mock election in 1964 and managed to secure the same result as Sir Alec Douglas-Home achieved on a national basis), giving ballroom dancing lessons to the juniors (those were the days!), getting out of games. (When I became Chairman of the National Playing Fields Association I did not reveal that when I left the playing field after my last game of compulsory rugger I went down on my knees in the changing room, and said, 'Dear Lord, so long as I do not have to play another game of rugby or football or cricket I promise never, ever, ever to complain about anything again so long as I live.' The Almighty has kept her side of the bargain. I have tried to keep mine.)

The theatre was my principal non-curricular enthusiasm. Our drama teacher reminded us constantly of Stanislavski's dictum that 'there are no small parts, only small actors', but

Under the Jumper

happily, from my point of view, didn't oblige me to put the dictum to the test and allowed me plum parts in the school plays. I repaid her generosity with suitably plummy performances. The *Petersfield Post* acclaimed my Malvolio ('Brandreth steals the show in Bedales *Twelfth Night*'), while Michael Hordern, whose daughter played Olivia, was possibly nearer the mark when he was overheard (by *my* parents) fulminating against 'the most appalling bit of amateur over-acting I have ever seen'.

My best friend, then as now, was Simon Cadell, a proper actor, whose Sherlock Holmes, aged 12, in my production of *A Study in Sherlock* was definitive. Simon and I were ludicrously middle-aged teenagers, who when we weren't listening to Noël Coward at Las Vegas were impersonating Flanagan and Allen Underneath the Arches. (If you've not heard of Flanagan and Allen, don't worry. They were old hat *then*.) Simon was two years younger than me but infinitely more sophisticated. I have never smoked and didn't touch alcohol until I went to university. At fourteen, Simon could blow perfect smoke rings and tell a Meursault from a Chardonnay at a hundred paces. When women wrote to him they wrote to the right man.

Simon was impatient to leave Bedales. He wanted to get into the real world. I am not sure that he was particularly happy at school. I believe I was happy, whatever 'happy' is. I was busy and content (I was probably content because I was busy) and, as I recall, fairly free of adolescent anguish. I am not given over much to introspection. This is a dangerous thing to admit, but I don't think it follows necessarily that deep down I'm shallow. I like to think it means that I have observed that *excessive* introspection can make one *overly* aware of personal shortcomings. We're all flawed, but does brooding about it help?

DEATH

'I'm not afraid to die. I just don't want to be there when it happens.'
Woody Allen

Before going off to boarding-school, one of the ways in which I kept myself busy-busy-busy in London was by going to church. I was a choir boy at Holy Trinity, Brompton Road, a choir boy at Saint Mary Abbots, Kensington Church Street, and a server at Saint Stephen's, Gloucester Road – simultaneously. My weekday evenings were given over to a round of choir practices and evensongs, my Satudays devoted to weddings (when the rate went up from two shillings to half-a-crown there was indeed rejoicing in the choir) and Sundays I spent ricocheting around Kensington, plunging in and out of cassocks and surplices from first communion to last compline.

St Stephen's was my chief delight because of the incense, because John Masefield and TS Eliot were regular worshippers (and I knew 'Sea Fever' and 'Macavity the Mystery Cat' by heart), and because Father Howard took me under his wing. He was small and round and bespectacled and, once, when nobody was looking, he let me try on his birreta. He also showed me my first coffin.

After the last service on a Sunday I would escort Father Howard around the church, holding the candle snuffer for him. At each altar he would genuflect, I would pass him the

snuffer, he would extinguish the candles, return the snuffer
to me, we would genuflect again and move on. One Sunday
we departed from our normal route and he led me through
the vestry to a tiny, sepulchrally dark chapel beyond. On a
trestle in the middle of the room was a bare coffin with large
orange candles at each corner. We knelt by the coffin, Father
Howard said a prayer, we snuffed the candles and came out.

As I pulled off my surplice I asked Father Howard, 'Was
that person dead?'

'No,' said Father Howard, 'he is very much alive, and he
will live for ever. That's the joy of death.'

I was eight when this happened. I was eighteen before I
attended a full funeral as a legitimate mourner.

During the pregnant pause between school and university I
spent much of the nine months in the United States, where I
had (and you have too) a range of relatives on both my
father's and my mother's side. I was teaching English at the
Park School in Baltimore and struggling to persuade a group
of fourteen year olds of the delights of Emily Dickinson (not
a very *happening* poet) when I was rescued from my travails
by a message brought to the classroom saying that my
Great-Aunt Polly had died in New York and my presence
was expected at the funeral.

The Greyhound bus got me to New York and the subway
took me to the darker part of Brooklyn where, with
difficulty, I located the McManus Funeral Parlor, arriving
shortly after the ceremony was due to begin. At the reception
desk an oleaginous manager, with the haughty and, at the
same time, ingratiating manner of an over-familiar *maître d'*,
asked for the name of my loved one and then led me through
a warren of panelled corridors to a small chapel where a few
wailers were gathered around an open coffin. I braced myself
and closed my eyes as I approached the casket. When I
opened them I let out an involuntary yelp. The lady sitting up
in the coffin was black and my recollection of Aunt Polly
(albeit I had met her only once) was that she was white. At

my cry the wailers turned up the volume and the *maître d'*
took me firmly by the elbow and pulled me out into the
hallway.

'What was the name of your loved one?' he hissed.

'Mrs McSkimming, Mrs Polly McSkimming.'

'Thank you,' he said with a heavy sigh.

Moments later I found myself in a larger, lighter, brighter
chapel of rest. This looked more like it. Indeed, even Aunt
Polly looked more like it. Messrs McManus had given my
aged aunt a remarkably youthful appearance. They had
curled her hair, rouged her cheeks, crammed her into her
wedding dress and given her a tartan sash for good measure.
(With a name like McSkimming that seemed appropriate.)
They had even blessed the bride with lipstick. 'Of course,' my
cousin Agnes confided, 'your great aunt never wore lipstick
in real life, but we believe it becomes her now.'

Soon after my arrival the formal obsequies began with the
Minister announcing that 'the service of last rites will be
performed by the Lodge of the Northern Star', at which
point six matrons in the robes of the Order filed in and
placed themselves in a semi-circle around the coffin. In turn
each recited a verse and tucked a flower inside the casket,
then they all broke into song. It was at this point that I was
overcome with nervous giggles. If and when this happens to
you, there are techniques for suppressing it: breathe slowly
and deeply, and jab your fingernails into the palm of your
hand as hard as you can while counting to ten. Whatever you
do don't catch the eye of a co-conspirator. At Great-Aunt
Polly's funeral my problem was compounded by being seated
next to Sloan Wilson, a writer who had recently married one
of my cousins and seemed intent on having the nervous
giggles too.

Sloan was the celebrated member of the family, having
written *The Man in the Gray Flannel Suit* and *A Summer
Place*, both of which had been made into movies. I was
drawn to him because of his celebrity, and then warmed to

him because he seemed good-humoured and wise. He was then the age I am now and I was exactly your age then. While they didn't all ring true to me at the time I don't know that I would quarrel now with Sloan's list of the things life had taught him:

1. Liquid shoe polish doesn't work.
2. A man who wants time to read and write must let the grass grow long.
3. Beware of people who are always well-dressed.
4. The hardest part of raising children is teaching them to ride bicycles. A father can run beside the bicycle or stand yelling directions while the child falls. A shaky child on a bicycle for the first time needs both support and freedom. The realisation that this is what the child will always need can hit hard.
5. Children go away and live their own lives, starting when they are about eighteen. Parents who accept this as a natural part of the order of things will see their grown children surprisingly often.
6. Friends are fun, but they are more dangerous than strangers. Strangers ask for a quarter for a cup of coffee, while friends ask for a thousand dollars, no questions asked if you're a *real* friend. Some friends also have a roving eye for your wife and daughters.
7. Despite all the advice about how to achieve connubial bliss, a happy marriage is usually an unearned miracle. The reasons why some people get on so well together are as mysterious as the reasons why other people fight.
8. When things break around the house, call a handyman. No intelligent man is capable of fixing anything unless he has made home repair his business.

I may have got the giggles at Great-Aunt Polly's funeral, but my laughter was nervous not mocking. The ritual was unfamiliar, a far cry from St Stephen's, Gloucester Road, no more or less absurd, just different. The wake was celebratory and could afford to be because Mrs McSkimming was an old lady who had lived a full life well. What more could one ask? Some deaths are described as untimely, as though others are timely. Her family accepted that her time had come.

Some people cannot reconcile themselves to a death, timely or otherwise. I had just started out on the public-speaking circuit when one of the circuit's most illustrious performers dropped down dead on the tennis court. Godfrey Winn was the highest-paid journalist of his day and much sought after by ladies' luncheon clubs. When the agency rang a club in Haslemere to break the sad news that Godfrey would not be appearing at their lunch on Friday because that was to be the day of his funeral, the club secretary protested, 'But he must come.'

'Sadly,' said the lady from the agency, 'he can't. We'll send you Mr Brandreth instead. He's very good and quite a bit cheaper than Mr Winn.'

'But we booked Mr Winn,' the club secretary insisted, 'he really has to come, you know, he signed the contract.'

'Yes, but you don't seem to understand: the poor man's *dead.*'

'That's easy for you to say,' retorted the club secretary, 'what you don't seem to understand is that I've had the menus printed.'

Godfrey and I were both with the speakers' agency owned and managed by Cyril Fletcher who, when a member of the audience died at the top table while I was speaking, chortled, 'We must use that on your billing: "With Brandreth they die laughing." ' Cyril, who has a deep faith and knows that God has a way of levelling the score (a lady once gave birth in the gallery when Cyril was playing Mother Goose) told me the story of another pantomime where the Boxing Day performance had to be cancelled because Widow Twankey suffered a fatal heart attack just as the curtain was set to rise. The front of house manager shuffled nervously onto the stage, 'Ladies and gentlemen, boys and girls, I am very sorry to have to inform you that this evening's performance cannot take place because one of the leading players has suffered a severe heart attack.'

In unison, the audience chorused back, 'Oh, no he hasn't!'

In New York in the sixties 'singing telegrams' were all the rage. An advertising executive was throwing a party to mark his fortieth birthday and, at the height of the festivities, the doorbell rang and the telegram boy from Western Union presented himself at the front door.

'Quiet everybody,' called the host. 'Here's a telegram and the boy's going to sing it to us.'

'I'd rather not,' said the boy.

'Go on,' cried the host, 'it's my birthday.'

'I'd rather not, if you don't mind,' pleaded the boy.

'I do mind,' insisted the host. 'It's my birthday, it's my party, it's my telegram. Sing it!'

The boy opened the cable, cleared his throat and sang: 'Trala, trala, trala, your sister Rose is dead!'

Why do we make jokes about death? Because we're frightened? Because the subject is still taboo? Because if we send it up we think we can keep it at bay? When I was your age morbid curiosity led me to visit Death Row at the Baltimore State Penitentiary. The assistant governor of the prison showed me the cell-on-wheels in which the condemned offender would be trundled towards the gas chamber. With a twinkle he invited me to step inside and 'try the pressure cooker for size'. He introduced me to a couple of the inmates awaiting execution and, extraordinarily, they joined in his joshing banter about 'cooking with gas' being preferable to 'the electric fry'.

I have every sympathy with those left behind who seek to make contact with those who have gone before. At around the time of Godfrey Winn's death I was working with a small publisher in Gerrard's Cross who produced a book by a Latvian psychologist, Dr Konstantin Raudive, who had discovered a technique for communicating with the dead and recording their voices on everyday audio tape. I took part in one of Dr Raudive's experiments and, sure enough, after an hour or five of patient recording a series of crackly cries reached us from the beyond. The voices spoke in Latvian, German, French and broken English. As a friend of the publisher, the Apostolic Nuncio Archbishop Cardinale, said, 'It is all very mysterious, but we know that the voices are there for everyone to hear.' As I write, I have just been listening again to one of the tapes and I must say it does sound very like Winston Churchill.

Unfortunately for the publisher and Dr Raudive, Churchill and James Joyce and (of all people) Sir John Barbirolli were remarkably taciturn when they did get through. We could only catch odd words and half-phrases, and, while the book caused a modest flurry of interest when it was published, the 'amazing breakthrough in electronic communication with the dead' turned into a nine-day wonder.

The reality of death is no laughing matter. My father took two years to die and it was veritable agony for him, both because of the pain and because he was not ready to go. The two hospices where he stayed off and on were a help, but not as much of a help as they thought and their publicity would have you believe. I know that even to whisper a doubt about the sanctity of the hospice movement is like casting aspersions on the Queen Mother or questioning Judi Dench's ability as an actress – some institutions CAN DO NO WRONG – but while a hospice may be right for many it was not entirely right for my father. When the Duchess of Kent came to call (which was sweet of her, I know) she and my poor frail dad appeared on the front page of the *Marylebone Mercury*. That's when he knew his number was up. And he didn't like it. In theory, of course, we have to accept the inevitable, but in practice some will still want to rage against the dying of the light, and the hushed bonhomie of the visitors combined with the seraphic serenity of the nuns can be jolly irritating if, in fact, you feel you're alive but not well and, despite having reached your three score year and ten, you've got more to offer and you'd like some extra time, PLEASE, in which to offer it.

Watching my father fade, and rally, and fade, and rally, and fade again, was heart-breaking and the only deeply unhappy experience I have known. I could not bear it for him, or for me, or for my brother or my sisters, or, most of all, for my mother. The horror of a good marriage is that there is this barbaric pay-off at the end.

Around the time my father died in 1982 I was starting to work on a play about the life of A A Milne, father of Christopher Robin and creator of Winnie the Pooh. For Alan Milne saying the long goodbye began when he was twelve: 'Farewell, Papa, with your brave, shy heart and your funny little ways; with your humour and your wisdom and your never-failing goodness: from now on we shall begin to grow out of each other. I shall be impatient, but you will be patient with me; unloving, but you will not cease to love me. "Well", you will tell yourself, "it lasted until he was twelve; they grow up and resent our care for them, they form their own ideas, and think ours old-fashioned. It is natural. But oh, to have that little boy again, whom I used to throw up to the sky, his face laughing down into mine –" And once, when he did this, his elbow, which he had put out at cricket, went out as he threw, and he had to catch me with one arm, and he told us the story, how often, and my brother and I would nudge each other, how often, and feel mocking and superior, as if *we* had never told a story more than once. But still, you had me until I was twelve, Papa, and if there was anything which you ever liked in me or of which you came to be proud, it was yours. Thank you, dear.'

ENERGY

'Energy is eternal delight!'
William Blake

Perhaps the crowning glory of my father's career at Oxford in the 1920s was his assault on the role of Old Manoa in a production of Milton's *Samson Agonistes* directed by a young Nevill Coghill. My father carried much of the role round in his head for the rest of his life and any domestic mishap, major or minor, was greeted with the sonorous refrain:

Come, come; no time for lamentation now,
Nor much more cause ...

In the 1960s Coghill's continuing claims to theatrical fame included his production of Marlowe's *Doctor Faustus* (with Richard Burton and Elizabeth Taylor), his rollicking musical version of Chaucer's *Canterbury Tales*, and his versified prologue to my production of Byron's *Cinderella*.

My Byron isn't your Byron. My Byron is Henry James Byron, Victorian journalist and comic playwright, whose 'fairy burlesque extravaganza' of *Cinderella, or The Lover, The Lackey and the Little Glass Slipper* was first presented at the Royal Strand Theatre, London, on 26 December 1860, and revived by yours truly at the Oxford Playhouse on

33

12 November 1968. I persuaded Professor Coghill to write a prologue simply by asking him. I persuaded Sir Michael Redgrave to perform the prologue on the opening night simply by asking him too.

I wrote to Sir Michael care of the Yvonne Arnaud Theatre in Guildford where, by odd coincidence, he had recently revived *Samson Agonistes*. I wrote at length, telling him how much I admired him, how his Uncle Vanya was definitive (true), telling him that Professor Coghill had composed the prologue entirely with him in mind (not quite true), telling him that what the undergraduates of Oxford needed in their midst right now was a huge, great, colossal, towering talent like his. Would he come, just for one night, I'd cover the train fare, please. Forty-eight hours later I received a telegram: 'DELIGHTED STOP REDGRAVE'.

On 12 November, with my silk bow-tie and my first night butterflies both in place, I made my way to Oxford Station to meet the great man's train. I had replied to Sir Michael's telegram with an effusive letter of thanks and detailed instruction, explaining that he would find me waiting for him at the ticket barrier. He wouldn't recognise me, but I would recognise him. Or so I thought. The train was crowded. The passengers poured out of the carriages onto the platform and surged through the barrier and away. There was no sign of Sir Michael. The last passenger handed in his ticket and the platform was bare. The curtain was going up in forty-five minutes and where was my star? I peered down the platform and there I saw him in the far distance, a huge frame in a dishevelled raincoat, carrying a little battered briefcase and looking about him with a somewhat vacant air. I ran towards him. He shuffled towards me.

'Sir Michael?'

'Yes?'

'Sir Michael!'

'Yes. Are you, er –'

'I'm Gyles, yes.'

'Oh good,' and his large, old face broke into a sweet smile.
'How are you?'

'Not well,' he sighed, 'Not at all well.'

Slowly, painfully slowly, we made our way to the waiting
taxi. Sir Michael explained that he felt unsteady and 'strange'
and that his voice had gone, 'completely gone'. At the stage
door, he said he thought a glass of port might help. Michèle
ran to the Gloucester Arms, bought a bottle (Cockburn's
Special Reserve) and brought it back. He wouldn't use the
dressing room we had provided. He preferred to stand in the
wings. He took a glass of port, gargled with it and swallowed
it down. He took another. And another. And one more. The
orchestra had finished the overture. An expectant hush had
fallen over the auditorium.

'You're on now, Sir Michael,' I whispered.

'I don't think I can do it,' he said.

'You're on!'

And the stooped, shambling figure stepped from the wings
onto the stage and into the spotlight and was *transformed*.
Tall, erect, strong, formidable. 'Ladies and gentlemen, good
evening!' the voice boomed, the audience cheered, the magic
happened.

That night he found the energy. Over the next fifteen
years, as Parkinson's Disease took a firmer grip of him,
finding the energy became increasingly difficult. At first no
one realised what was wrong. One day we were having lunch
at the old Empress Restaurant in Grosvenor Square and his
head simply fell forward onto the table. He seemed drunk,
but he wasn't. He invited Michèle and me to lunch at his new
house in Lower Belgrave Street and, showing us round,
flopped down onto the stairs. He was bewildered, 'What is
happening?'

He loathed first nights. We witnessed the worst of them. In
1971 I was starting out in publishing and editing a series of
drama scripts including a play by William Trevor called *The
Old Boys*. It was presented by Bernard Miles at the Mermaid

with Michael in the lead. Because by the dress rehearsal he didn't have a grasp of the lines, for the first night the management equipped him with a hearing-aid through which he could be prompted. Sadly, the audience could hear the prompter better than Michael could. Is it my imagination or did we also hear the local minicab service? We certainly heard a cacophony of electric squawks and burrs and, when the apparatus fell from Michael's ear and disintegrated and scattered in pieces around him, it seemed to symbolise the heartrending end of a glorious career.

It wasn't the end, but the beginning of the end, and at least it got him to the Hospital for Nervous Diseases and a correct diagnosis. At last he knew what was wrong, even if he didn't like it. He described this period of his life as 'a grey expanse, with intermittent shafts of light'. When we met, his mind would come and go, he would talk of the glory days, of Vanessa and her politics ('It gives strength to her acting, it doesn't detract'), of Edith Evans. He always came back to Edith Evans. 'If you are going to play Orlando, you must *love* your Rosalind! You know, I made love to Edith on the night that Vanessa was born.' Acting with Edith, he said, 'was like being in your mother's arms, like knowing how to swim, like riding a bicycle. You're safe.... For the first time in my life acting with her in *As You Like It*, I felt completely unselfconscious. Acting with her made me feel, oh, it's so easy. You don't start acting, she told me, until you stop *trying* to act. It doesn't leave the ground until you don't have to think about it.... For the first time, on stage or off, I felt completely free.'

Laurence Olivier knew about energy, none more so. After their triumph together in *Uncle Vanya* at Chichester (the recording of that production would certainly find its way to my desert island) Olivier invited Redgrave to join him for the opening season of the National. Sir Michael was Claudius to Peter O'Toole's Hamlet under Sir Laurence's direction. For the first time, Redgrave couldn't command the energy. In rehearsal Olivier admonished him, 'When you came on as Macbeth, it was as if you were saying, "Fuck you, I *am* Macbeth." As Claudius you are *dim*.'

Ask John Gielgud what makes the so-called 'star' and he will suggest: 'Energy, an athletic voice, a well-graced manner, certainty of execution, some unusually fascinating originality of temperament. Vitality, certainly, and an ability to convey an impression of beauty or ugliness as the part demands, as well as authority and a sense of style.'

Not that it would make it to my desert island, but I have a charming recording of Cicely Courtneidge stopping the show (the show was *Gay's the Word*, the year 1951) with a knock 'em down Ivor Novello/Alan Melville number, 'Vitality':

Vitality!
It matters more than personality, originality or topicality,
For it's vitality that made all those topliners top!
Vitality!
They each had individuality but in reality their speciality was a vitality
Enough to make hits out of flops!

If I look down the happily varied list of star performers I have seen on stage, in cabaret or one-man shows, the common denominator is energy. Maurice Chevalier, Joyce Grenfell, Flanders and Swann, Donald Wolfit, Michael MacLiammoir, Emlyn Williams, Alec McCowen, Barbra Streisand, Liza Minelli, Ken Dodd, Bruce Forsyth. (Yes, my boy, Bruce Forsyth. It was the same with Liberace. We went to mock, we stayed to praise. Style, charm, clarity of purpose, energy.) Marlene Dietrich brought her energy to the stage door with her. When we were teenagers, Simon Cadell and I sat in the gods at the Golders Green Hippodrome to witness one of the first of her farewell tours. After the show we carried on cheering as she teetered on top of her limousine distributing signed photographs to the adoring fans. A policeman and I helped her off the car roof. Yes, for a brief moment in time, I held Marlene in my arms ...

Twenty-five years after Michael Redgrave opened the Yvonne Arnaud Theatre in Guildford with a season of Milton and Turgenev, I made my début there with Bonnie Langford in *Cinderella*. I played Bonnie's dad, Baron Hardup (a dry-run for life at the Treasury really) and our Buttons was a bright-eyed, bushy-tailed TV presenter-turned-trooper called Mark Curry. Mark had first appeared with Bonnie in *Babes in the Wood* when they were both about eleven and he told me how on the first night, Babette Langford, Bonnie's indomitable mum, had come up to him in the wings moments before he and Bonnie were due to go on stage.

'Now, Mark,' said Mrs Langford, 'when you get out onto that stage what are you going to do?'

Mark couldn't think what Mrs Langford meant. 'I don't know,' he stammered.

'Come along, now, Mark. When you get out there what are you going to *do*?'

'Remember my lines?' he tried hopefully.

'No, no, Mark. What are you going to *do*?'

'Not bump into Bonnie?'

'Don't be silly, Mark,' tut-tutted Mrs L. 'Mark, when you get out onto that stage, you're going to *sparkle*!'

And sparkle, Bonnie did – aged four in *Gone with the Wind* at Drury Lane ('There are only two things that need cutting in this show,' said Noël Coward. 'The first number in the second half and that child's throat'), aged eleven in *Babes in the Wood* and, certainly, I can vouch for it, unfailingly thirteen times a week (twice nightly with three shows on Saturday) when we played together in *Cinderella* at Guildford and Wimbledon. It was a phenomenon to witness at close quarters. When she made her entrance she ran on, hit her spot and then let her eyes take in every seat in the auditorium from the left-hand of the back row of the upper circle, to the last seat at the right-hand end of the front row. I watched her eyes at work and I marvelled. The audience marvelled too. Most came with reservations, not expecting to fall for an all-singing, all-dancing Violet Elizabeth Bott. They came away pleasantly surprised. Peter Bowles said, amazed, 'She's remarkably sexy.'

I appeared on Russell Harty's chat show. It was live and we stood together in the wings waiting for the signature tune. The moment he heard it Russell began to leap about, doing an eccentric dance, punching the air with his arms, flailing about as he worked himself into a frenzy. When the cue came, he stopped quite still for a single beat and then bounced brightly onto the set.

When I worked on a series with David Frost I marvelled at his ability to spring into action fresh from an overnight flight and a chilled bottle of Chablis. Then I stood by him once, just before he was due to go on, and watched him look at the studio clock and count himself down, 'Ten, nine, eight, seven ... three, two, one, I'm on!' And he was.

A few months ago I had dinner with Richard Nixon. He had just turned eighty, but the energy seemed undimmed. He was still playing the crowd, working the room. Whether illusory or real, it was as Churchill said of the company of his 'great contemporaries', 'one did feel after a talk with these men that things were simpler and easier.' Nixon said that the energy had been drained from George Bush and, quite simply, the electorate sensed it and moved on.

FE Smith, First Earl of Birkenhead, was one of Churchill's great contemporaries and a folkloric figure in the Brandreth household because my father was born and bred in Hoylake and his father, like FE (though, of course, not at all like FE), had practised briefly at the Liverpool bar. FE's prodigious energy was awe-inspiring and puts him in a league, I reckon, with Lloyd George and Churchill and Thatcher. Churchill noted that FE was consistent and *persistent*: In every affair, public or personal, if he was with

you on the Monday, you would find him the same on the
Wednesday, and on the Friday when things looked blue, he
would still be marching forward with strong reinforcements.
The opposite type of comrade or ally is so very common that
I single this out as a magnificent characteristic. He loved
pleasure; he was grateful for the gift of existence; he loved
every day of his life. But no one could work harder. From his
youth he worked and played with might and main. He had a
singular power of concentration, and five or six hours of
thought upon a particular matter was always within his
compass. He possessed what Napoleon praised, the mental
power '*de fixer les objets longtemps sans être fatigué.*'

Yes, Napoleon had it too.

FRAILTIES

'I have more flesh than another man, and therefore more frailty.'
Falstaff in *Henry IV, Part I*

I can never have my fill of FE Smith stories. He could be charming:

Mr Justice Darling: And who is George Robey?
FE: Mr George Robey is the Darling of the music-halls, m'ld.

He could be caustic:

Judge: I have read your case, Mr Smith, and I am no wiser now than I was when I started.
FE: Possibly not, my lord, but far better informed.

He had a nerve that was breathtaking. The most celebrated of his courtroom rallies took place with the well-intentioned but long-winded Judge Willis in Southwark County Court. A boy had been run over by a tram and was suing the tramway company for damages on the grounds that the accident had led to his blindness. The judge was affected by the lad's plight: 'Poor, poor boy! Blind! Put him on a chair so the jury can see him.'
FE was appearing for the tramway company and

protested: 'Perhaps your honour would like to have the boy passed round the jury box?'

'That is a most improper remark,' reproved the judge.

'It was provoked by a most improper suggestion,' retorted FE.

Judge Willis paused and then offered the outspoken counsel a lofty rebuke: 'Mr Smith, have you ever heard of a saying by Bacon – the great Bacon – that youth and discretion are ill-wedded companions?'

'Indeed I have, your honour,' came the instant reply. 'And has your honour ever heard of a saying by Bacon – the great Bacon – that a much-talking judge is like an ill-tuned cymbal?'

'You are extremely offensive,' spluttered the hapless Willis.

'As a matter of fact,' demurred FE, 'we both are; the difference between us is that I'm trying to be and you can't help it.'

On another occasion the same unfortunate judge turned testily to FE and remarked, 'What do you suppose I am on the bench for, Mr Smith?' FE's rejoinder was immediate and devastating: 'It is not for me, your honour, to attempt to fathom the inscrutable workings of Providence.'

Churchill was of the opinion that while FE was an effective Commons performer (it is no exaggeration to say that his maiden speech 'made' his parliamentary reputation), and even more impressive when he sat on the Woolsack as Lord Chancellor, he was at his most formidable as a speaker on the public platform. At an election meeting FE was confronted by a garrulous heckler. FE suggested the man remove his cap while putting his question.

'I'll take my boots off if you like,' called out the heckler.

'Ah,' sighed FE, 'I knew you'd come here to be unpleasant.'

On a similar occasion he was coming towards his peroration: 'Now, ladies and gentlemen, let me tell you exactly what the government has done for all of you.'

'Nothing!' shouted a woman from the back of the hall.

'My dear lady,' said FE without pause, 'the light in this hall is so dim as to prevent a clear sight of your undoubted charms, so that I am unable to say with certainty whether you are a virgin, a matron, or a widow, but in any case I will guarantee to prove that you are wrong. If you are a virgin flapper, we have given you the vote; if you are a wife, we have increased employment and reduced the cost of living; if you are a widow, we have given you a pension. And if you are none of these, but are foolish enough to be a tea drinker, we have reduced the tax on sugar!'

President Woodrow Wilson is reputed to have asked FE what, in his opinion, was the 'trend of the modern English undergraduate'. FE is supposed to have replied, 'Steadily towards women and drink, Mr President.'

If he said it I imagine he said it with approval because his own tendency was in a similar direction. As you know, I like to quote the little verse by (I think) Edna St Vincent Millay:

> I burn the candle at both ends;
> It will not last the night;
> But, ah, my foes, and, oh, my friends –
> It gives a lovely light.

Churchill reported that FE 'burned all his candles at both ends. His physique and constitution seemed to be capable of supporting indefinitely every form of mental and physical exertion. When they broke the end was swift.' FE died in 1930, aged 58. The drink killed him.

In *Enemies of Promise* (1938) Cyril Connolly anatomised those distractions that prevent writers of real talent from achieving their potential. In the corridors of Westminster his list may ring bells. It included alcohol and casual sex, worldly success, 'the pram in the hall', conversation and journalism. As a new boy at the Commons, I would add answering the telephone to the list.

There was a week last year when I received more than six

hundred calls. Admittedly, it was an exceptional week. The
American presidential campaign was at its height and word
had got out that I am an old friend of Bill Clinton. You didn't
know, son? I'm not surprised. I didn't know either until I
heard it from the *National Enquirer*. Apparently, in an
interview about his time as a Rhodes Scholar at Oxford, the
Governor of Arkansas had mentioned my name. As a
consequence my telephone hardly stopped ringing with
hungry newshounds on the line demanding to know more
about the Brandreth-Clinton salad days.

To give them their due, they were offering ready cash for
the right kind of reminiscence. Unfortunately, I have
absolutely no recollection of young Clinton, which is a
shame because I could have used the money. (This isn't a
complaint about the remuneration offered to MPs, more a
reflection of the fact that I appear to have run my domestic
economy much as dear old Jim Callaghan ran the country's
and I have not found the NatWest as malleable as the IMF.) I
met a girl who did remember Bill from Oxford. 'What was he
like?' I asked. 'He was *gorgeous*,' she said. 'Just think,'
mused Michèle, 'he was gorgeous then and he's President of
the United States now. You're a backbench MP now and you
weren't even gorgeous then. Something went wrong
somewhere.'

Even a homely backbencher who can't remember the right
Yank at Oxford is constantly being preyed on by the press
for 'a quick quote', on this, that and nothing in particular.
During the week last year when I monitored the calls, a
malicious piece appeared in *The Times* implying that the
Prime Minister was having/had had some sort of breakdown.
I received more than one press call along the lines of:

'Would you like to talk about the PM?'

'Not really.'

'Why not?'

'Because I haven't got anything special to say.'

'Does that mean you're unavailable for comment?'

'Good grief, no. I think the PM's marvellous.'

'Why don't you want to talk about him then?'

'You misunderstand me. I'm very happy to talk about him.'

'Well?'

'Well, what?'

'Well, how is he then?'

'He seems fine.'

'What do you mean he *seems* fine. Is there something wrong with him?'

'No, he's fine, but I'm just a backbencher, not his doctor.'

'Aha! So you think he should see a doctor. Can I quote you?'

The first mistake is letting the media take the initiative. My constituents frequently ask why they read and hear only what the extremists have to say. I tell them it's because Yeats was right and the best lack all conviction while the worst are full of passionate intensity. We reasonable folk, middle-of-the-road men and women, mainstream and moderate, are sitting back convinced that common sense must prevail, while the madmen and mavericks are out there, sound-biting the hand that feeds them, peddling their line to anyone who will listen – and there are plenty who will.

The lesson was brought home to me soon after the election when, along with a dozen other tyro Tories, I went to a private briefing with the Chancellor of the Exchequer. The meeting was instructive and constructive and, although no one said so, I assumed confidential. Twenty-four hours later I read a highly coloured account of it in the press. Clearly one of our number had trundled down the Treasury steps and sought out the nearest hack. No doubt it makes for good copy, but I am not sure it makes for good government. How can colleagues exchange views, argue points, float ideas, have genuine debate, if they have constantly to watch their words in case what they say may be reported, and reported through a distorting filter?

Remember, my son, a good journalist is a good journalist first, second and last. He can't be your best friend as well. And if he is, either you're being fooled or he's not the journalist you thought he was.

Seeing your name in print is not necessarily a mark of success, and extensive coverage, while possibly gratifying at the time, may turn out to be excessive coverage in the long run. I have counselled more than one aspiring Minister of State to decline invitations to be 'profiled', however sympathetically. It may lead to familiarity, but we know what that breeds. Column inches do not a leader make. When John Major became Prime Minister he probably had the thinnest press cutting file of any senior member of the Cabinet. I suspect the same was true of Margaret Thatcher in 1976.

There is no obligation on MPs to return telephone calls from the press. However, there is an expectation that they will answer letters from their constituents.

As I write this, our window cleaner has arrived and he is telling me he has just come from the local presbytery where he left the monsignor finishing a hearty breakfast of toast, Woodbines and whiskey.

'I smoke and I drink,' explained the monsignor, 'because I'm driven to it by all the problems.'

'But, surely,' said the window cleaner laying down his leather, 'surely, as a man of God, you don't have problems.'

'Of course, *I* don't have problems,' sighed the monsignor. 'It's my *flock* who have problems and they keep bringing them to me. I'm drinking and smoking for them.'

I know the feeling. Week in, week out, come recess or recession, the letters still pour in: over thirty on a good day, over seven hundred on the worst. Maybe it's because I'm so new (maybe it's because I'm so naïve), but I still feel an obligation to reply.

I sat down in the Members Tea Room recently with an old boy (my idea of a proper Tory backwoodsman, and there are disappointingly few of them left), who couldn't see his toasted tea-cake for the mountain of mail he had just collected from the postroom. He told me that when he first arrived at the House in the 1950s he could clear all his correspondence in under twenty minutes with personal handwritten notes, penned in the Library. 'Dear Bishop, Lady Wildbore and I will be *delighted* to join you for sherry on Friday. Yours, etc....' (Now the Bishops require very different replies. 'Dear Bishop Jerry, I fully understand your reservations about testing at Key Stage 3, particularly in relation to technology. Let me explain ...')

There are those MPs (and not just backwoodsmen) who advertise the fact that they won't take on council housing cases, or indeed other matters that are properly the responsibility of the appropriate local authority, but I feel, whatever the problem, you can't say no, you must try. Even if all you can do in too many cases is offer sympathy and a photocopied ministerial response, with the odd one you can make a difference, and with all you get at least a flavour of the concerns that are pressing on a portion of our fellow citizens.

In my first year at Westminster my principal enemy proved to be the clock. It is alarmingly easy to spend a day, a week, a month, running non-stop in front of an ever-encroaching avalanche of meetings, correspondence and phone calls – all individually essential, but cumulatively an almighty barrier to any in-depth reading, research or (heaven help me!) thought. I believe Peter Walker when he was a minister insisted that at least half an hour a day be kept clear in his diary simply for *thinking*.

Nowadays it isn't only members of parliament who are drowning in unsolicited correspondence. The humblest regional TV weather-girl is solicited daily for a prize to raffle, a promise to auction or a recipe to reproduce in the zillionth charity celebrity cookbook. John Cleese has resolved the dilemma. If you write to him this is the reply you will receive:

'Thank you for your recent letter. The problem is this. For some time, I have been struggling to create a routine whereby I have enough time to pursue my own interests. Unfortunately, I find – and I'm not exaggerating – that I've almost no time for my own major activities, like writing, because I have a constant stream of meetings and mail and telephone calls to attend to, eighty per cent of which derive from other folks' attempts to involve me in their projects, which – while splendid and very worthwhile – are still not as essentially interesting to me as my own. So, I'm afraid I'm giving a blanket 'No' to all requests for the forseeable future, in the hope that I can discharge all my other obligations and then actually be able to focus on my own projects for a time. Good luck.'

At dinner the other evening I asked Lord King, the President of British Airways, what single quality a successful leader needed most and he said, 'Luck – and energy. His own – and other people's.' If you put the same question to your cousin Sloan Wilson he would tell you that 'success in almost any field depends more on energy and drive than it does on intelligence; this is why we have so many stupid leaders.'

You, my boy, are lucky: you have intelligence. You also have energy and drive. To succeed in worldly terms (and it isn't compulsory, but it is available and, in this country, it is available to all), to achieve in almost any field of endeavour, you will also need concentration, staying power, singleness of purpose. And a little gall.

GALL

'Gall: effrontery, brashness, brass, cheek, confidence, crust, face, nerve, presumption.'

Webster's Collegiate Thesaurus

It was my friend Noel Davis who introduced me to *chutzpah*, not as the Yiddish equivalent of gall, but when I said in passing one day that there were no sympathetic Jewish characters in Shakespeare.

'Nonsense,' said Noel, 'think of *Henry IV*.'

'Who's Jewish in *Henry IV*?'

'Chutzpah, or course,' said Noel, 'Harry Chutzpah!'

Noel also introduced me to the Chinese waiter in *King Lear*. He appears only fleetingly. Lear calls him on in Act I Scene 3: 'Come hither, Ho!'

Then there was the story of the old actor, a *prima donna* of the bull-queen variety, who when told there wasn't a part to suit his temperament or style in *King Lear*, flourished his copy of the New Arden Shakespeare in front of the director triumphantly and declared (kindly assume a Kenneth Williams   voice for this bit): 'There is! There is! Look at the list of characters. What does it say on the bottom line? "A *camp* near Dover!"'

Naturally, it's the way he tells them. Nobody tells them better and nobody has more of them to tell. Noel is funny (outrageously, consistently, tremendously funny), thoughtful, courteous, camp (though these days more James Robertson-Justice than Julian Clary), a wonderful worker and the best of friends. Together we ran the Oxford Theatre Festival between 1974 and 1976 and put on eight plays, seven one-man shows, four concerts, six fringe companies, ten lunchtime lectures, five tours, three West End transfers and one *Evening Standard* Play of the Year. It wasn't all plain sailing, but when it was at its worst Noel was at his best. On one of our darkest nights he took us both off to the Elizabeth Restaurant in St Aldates ('One would not want to eat there too often – who could afford to? – but it is always an excitement to go there, and the proprietor and waiters know it.' *Good Food Guide*, 1973.) Noel ordered a magnum of the Château Latour 49 at £26 (that was a week's salary in 1974) and, as we charged and clinked our glasses, he defied the gods, 'Fuck 'em, darling, fuck 'em!'

(Oddly, this scene came back to me towards the end of last year when I was having lunch with Norman Lamont at 11 Downing Street. The vocabulary was more restrained (much), and the sentiments were implied not expressed, but as I explained to the Chancellor that, in my eyes, the problem with the ERM was that it had turned out to be a straitjacket while what we needed was a truss, we raised our glasses of Threshers' non-vintage best to the future and the spirit of looser corsetry.)

The Oxford Theatre Festival came about because I wanted to put on plays and the Oxford Playhouse, having wilfully rid itself of Frank Hauser's (justly) acclaimed Meadow Players, needed some middle-brow fare that would put bums on seats and restore some of the lustre that had been lost with Frank (whose leading artistes had included Judi Dench, Leo McKern, Alan Badel).

Over lunch at the Tackley in the High Street (where they used to flambée your dish at your table: veal with brandy, cream, mushrooms and a pleasant aroma of lighter fuel; unthinkable now; delicious then), the tough old boot who

ran the Playhouse put her hand on mind and said, 'If you can
find the plays, and you can find the stars, and you can find
the money, you can have the theatre.'

I told her I could and I would. And the message, my boy, is
if you think you can you will, so long as you've got the gall, a
copy of the *Spotlight* casting directory, a typewriter and a
handful of first class stamps.

My first letter went to Rita Tushingham, a considerable
film star in the sixties, from *A Taste of Honey* to *Doctor
Zhivago* via *Girl with Green Eyes* and *The Knack*. Would
she care to play the title role in Bernard Shaw's *Saint Joan* at
the 1974 Oxford Theatre Festival? She thought she might.
We met. She thought she would. I wrote to Sir John
Clements, who had just completed his last season as director
of the Chichester Festival Theatre. How did he feel about
playing the Earl of Warwick? He felt he was too old, but if I
hadn't yet settled on a director for the piece, could he be
considered? And what did I think of his stepson, John
Standing, as the Dauphin? Excellent. Excellent.

I wrote to Ian Carmichael. What would he say to a stage
version of Oscar Wilde's *Lord Arthur Savile's Crime*? He'd
say No, but if I'd care to trundle up to Mill Hill on the jolly
old tube he'd meet me at the station in the Roller and we
could chinwag over other possibilities and have a spot of
lunch. He wanted to revive Benn Levy's *Springtime for
Henry*, a high comedy (neither comedy nor farce – tricky)
and Barbara Murray would be the ideal leading lady. Done.

I wrote to Sir Ralph Richardson and made a pilgrimage to
his house in Regent's Park. Number One Chester Terrace
was a house in the grand manner. Sir Ralph had a play, a
new play, a ver' strange, ver' cu-rious new play, deah boy.
Patrick Garland had found it for him. Ralph was a
missionary. The rest of the cast were animals. Anna Massey
would make a ver' clever giraffe, don't you think? Sets in the
style of Douanier Rousseau. Hey-ho, cocky, if you do *The
Missionary* I'm going to be working for you this summer ...

I was finding the plays, I was finding the stars. What about
the money? I bought *Who's Who*. I needed someone
entrepreneurial, someone different, someone with money. I
worked through the As. The first person I wrote to was
Jeffrey Archer. He was the youngest MP in the Commons,
the member for Louth, and best known for having reunited
the Beatles for an Oxfam benefit. Yes, said Jeffrey,
intriguing. Some good names. Sir Ralph is extraordinary,
*extra*ordinary. Jeffrey's favourite actress, of course, was
Celia Johnson. So talented. So under-rated. Why oh why
wasn't she a dame? He'd spoken to Ted about it. Get Celia
Johnson and you've got your money.

Simon Cadell's father, a distinguished agent, suggested
James Bridie's *Daphne Laureola* might suit Miss Johnson. I
wrote. A postcard came back from Mrs Peter Fleming, Mer-
rimoles House, Nettlebed, Near Oxford. Yes, she'd love to.

Before I could get back to Jeffrey, who had given me a
range of telephone numbers, in the Boltons, in Whitehall, in
Louth, and told me to contact him at any time, day or night,
any time, I received a letter from Ray Cooney, arch-farceur
with ambitions to go legit. Was I looking for a partner? If so,
I'd found one.

Ray was bald and slight and energetic and, thanks to *Move
Over Mrs Markham, Don't Stay for Breakfast* and sundry
other classics of the genre, rich. He was also determined to
present Ralph Richardson and Celia Johnson in the West
End, especially Celia, because nobody could get Celia to say
yes to anything, but I had, so if I was interested we could do a
deal. He'd bank-roll the Oxford Theatre Festival in return
for any West End transfers. I'd get a share of the profits.
(Benet, if you learn nothing else from this book, remember
this: never take a share of the profits. There won't be any.
The only share that has meaning is a share of the gross.
Frankly, if you've absorbed that you can throw the book
away.)

I got more than a deal from Ray. I got an 'assistant'. To

keep a close eye on this theatrical *wunderkind* (I was 25) and an even closer eye on the accounts (we were set to spend £100,000) Ray produced Noel, a forty-something actor-turned-producer and walking *Spotlight*. From start to finish Noel was Ray's man, but from the first moment we set eyes on one another I knew he was my ally.

And I needed an ally because no sooner had the deal been done than everything began to go wrong. We were working out of Michèle's and my basement flat at Clarence Gate Gardens, off Baker Street. (TS Eliot had once lived there. The hall porter would occasionally show American students around. 'And this is where the celebrated poet, GH Elliott, used to reside ...') The telephone rang. 'Hello. It's Celia Fleming here.' She seemed to be telephoning from a garden. You could hear birds in the background. I could picture the trug over her arm and the gardening gloves and the secateurs in the hand that wasn't holding the 'phone. 'I'm frightfully sorry, Mr Brandreth, but I don't think it'll do.'

My mouth was already dry. 'What won't do?'

'The play. It really won't do. I read it again last night. And it's so dated. I'm sure Edith was marvellous, but Edith's Edith. It just won't do.'

'But –'

'I *am* sorry.' A lawnmower had started up. 'The trouble is no one's writing my kind of plays any more. Why can't people write like Noël and Terry nowadays? Willie's the only one who comes anywhere near. I am so – *very* – sorry. Do read the play again. I'm sure you'll agree. It just won't do.'

I told Noel, my Noel. We told Michèle. We didn't tell Ray. 'Who's Willie?' said Michèle. 'William Douglas-Home,' said Noel. I reached for *Who's Who*. I wrote to him that night. Did he have a play that might suit Celia Johnson? It arrived by return post. The title seemed ominous. It was called *In the Red*. It was a light comedy about the travails of a bank manager and his stockbroker-belt wife. It went to Nettlebed by special delivery.

'Celia Fleming here.' She was indoors. Did she have a gin in her hand? Could I hear ice? Was she about to play Bridge? 'I've read Willie's piece. It's *very* funny. I think we'll do it, don't you? What about the bank manager? Is John Clements too old? What about Michael Hordern? He'd be perfect.'

Having been to school with his daughter I had kept Michael Hordern's home address in my book for more than a decade against this very eventuality. I dropped the script, with covering note, through his letter box at about midnight. For seventy-two hours we heard nothing. Then the telephone rang.

'Celia Fleming here.' She was in the hallway now. Or was she in the drawing room, standing by the piano, gazing out over the lawn, watching Lucy set up the croquet things? 'Look, I'm frightfully sorry. Michael Hordern's just been on to me. He thinks it's a dreadful play. He says it's crude and obvious.' The bastard must have remembered my Malvolio, after all. 'I'm so very sorry Mr Brandreth. He's adamant he won't do it. And he thinks I shouldn't do it either. He's probably right. I hope you'll understand.'

I understood. Willie understood. Michèle and I went to East Meon and stayed the night. We arrived late. He offered us bread and cheese and shambled around the kichen, affecting to be totally lost. He attempted to slice the bread using the blunt edge of the bread-knife. Michèle saw through the ploy, but took over all the same. William and I went to his study and flicked through his unperformed works. There was nothing that was right. We munched our bread and cheese, drained our glasses, and went up to bed. As his bedside reading William took with him a biography of Sybil Hathaway, the Dame of Sark, who throughout the German occupation of her island stayed valiant, defiant and heartwarmingly British.

At breakfast, he said, 'There might be something in this.' He set to work that morning and five and a half days after writing 'The drawing room of the Seigneurie on Sark' he penned the words 'The Curtain Falls' in time to catch the start of the two o'clock race at Newbury. The script reached me on Monday. I got it to Celia on Tuesday. She said yes on Wednesday. We issued a press announcement on Thursday and that was that. Celia Johnson as the Dame of Sark, with Tony Britton, perfect as the professional-soldier-with-a-tender-heart-despite-the-Nazi-uniform, played to capacity in Oxford, transferred to Wyndham's and then to the Duke of York's (where Anna Neagle took over). We had a hit.

I don't believe we'd have had a hit with *The Missionary*, with or without Sir Ralph, though I'm damned sure Anna Massey would have been the best bloody giraffe to grace the West End stage since Michael Saint-Denis presented André Obey's *Noah* with John Gielgud and friends at the New Theatre in 1935. Sir Ralph was right to have misgivings about *The Missionary*. He was equally well advised to decline the role of Goya in an epic that came my way (via Peter Coe, I think) and featured the great artist towards the end of his life when he had gone blind. It was a powerful piece, but, as I recall, it required the audience to shut their eyes whenever Goya himself was on stage to fully share the sensation of his blindness. Sir Ralph twigged that the more conscientious members of the audience would consequently miss much of his performance.

We replaced Sir Ralph with Geraldine McEwan in a revival of *The Little Hut*, André Roussin's desert island high comedy (neither comedy nor farce, tricky). This was Ray Cooney's idea and allowed Noel to invite every black actor in London and under thirty to come to our basement and take his clothes off. 'The native is a loin-cloth part,' explained Noel, 'I'm sure you understand.' Happily, the actors did (even if our neighbours didn't) and eventually we cast Olu Jacobs, a fine actor and equally fine figure of a man, in the role.

We had been looking for a middle-brow season. It seemed to be verging on the lightweight now, so, between the high comedies, I was allowed to squeeze in *Waiting for Godot*. It was the first revival since Peter Hall's original production in 1955. I looked up Samuel Beckett's address in *Who's Who* and wrote to him. He wrote back saying yes, particularly if Patrick Magee would direct. He would. And did. Brilliantly.

We appeared to be back on track and then Rita Tushingham pulled out. She had been offered a movie in Israel. We'd have to release her. She was sorry. She knew we'd understand. We understood all right. We released her and scrawled offensive remarks all over her entry in *Spotlight*.

'We will, never, ever, ever, EVER use that cow again,' I bawled.

'Until we need her,' said Noel.

Saint Joan without Tush was *Hamlet* without the Prince, especially as we'd lined up Sir John and John Standing and James Villiers and Noel Willman and Charles Dance and heaven knows who else entirely on the strength of her name. This time we told Ray. And we also told him our solution. We had enough stars for one season. Let's just go for a good actress, unknown but absolutely right (Michèle's idea and, by happy chance, a client of Simon Cadell's father): Frances de la Tour.

'Good God,' spluttered Ray, 'I'm not putting on George Bernard Shaw's *Saint Joan* with Frances de la Number Three Tour. I want a name, a canopy name.' We trawled *Spotlight*. Eileen Atkins, not available. Diana Rigg, not available. Maggie Smith, not available. Anna Massey.

'We're looking for a martyr, not a giraffe.'

'She's good.'

'I know, but ...'

Janet Suzman, not available. Susan Hampshire, not available. Jane Asher, not available. Anna Calder-Marshall.

'Who?'

'Never mind ... Billie Whitelaw. How about Billie Whitelaw?'

I called Miss Whitelaw's agent. I called Miss Whitelaw. I
was a friend of Samuel Beckett. (Well, a pen-friend.) Sir John
Clements wanted her above all others. (Actually I hadn't yet
broken the news to him about Tush's flight to Israel, but that
was to be my next call.) Could she sleep on it? In her sleep,
she must have heard voices. They told her to say Yes.

'Sir John, I have bad news and good news. The bad news is
that we've lost Rita Tushingham. The good –'

'Get on a train at once,' he barked, 'at once. Bring
Spotlight. We'll sort it out today.'

'But Sir John –'

'At once!'

It was a Sunday morning at ten. By noon I was perched on
the little balcony of the Clements' flat on the front at
Brighton. Sir John was fixing us schlerosis-sized gins and
tonic and his dear frail wife, Kay Hammond, was trying
slowly and painfully to explain to me that she had been
something of a star herself before she had her stroke. 'I
know,' I said, 'I loved *Genevieve*.' (That was Kay Kendall,
you fool. Kay Hammond, *Blithe Spirit*. Remember?)

'Lunch first,' said Sir John, 'then work.' Lunch was served
in a small alcove off the drawing room and brought in by an
elderly servant in an improbable wig (was it the same lady
who waited at table in the Redgrave household?) who was
summoned by an electric bell whose button was discreetly
positioned by Miss Hammond's place at table. Unfortunately, while the bell made a dreadful racket all over the
flat, the servant in the kitchen couldn't hear it and Sir John
had to go and fetch her between every course.

Over coffee, I broke the good news.

'I've secured Billie Whitelaw.'

'But you can't have.' He was open-jawed.

'I have.'

'No, no, no. You haven't.' He was wild-eyed.

'I have.'

'But you *cannot* have recast the title part without

consulting the director.'

I had. It was wrong. It was a mistake. And even now, more than twenty years after the event, my palms go damp as I think back to the call I made to explain to Miss Whitelaw and her agent that I had failed to consult the director, that Sir John loved Miss Whitelaw, both as a person and as a performer, but that for him as Saint Joan she was wrong, all wrong, that the fault was mine, all mine, and that Miss Julia Foster, a younger actress, in Mr Cooney's eyes a film star (*Alfie*) and a canopy name following her West End triumph in *Lulu*, would be giving her Saint Joan at the Oxford Theatre Festival.

The production was not an unmitigated disaster. There were problems. Michèle (pregnant with you by now) and I were still sizing the set at 3.00 am on the day of the dress rehearsal, and the *éclat* of the first night when it arrived (forty-eight hours later than advertised) was clouded by the theatre management's insistence on showing advertisements on the safety curtain during the interval (including one featuring our Earl of Warwick as a chinless wonder smoking Benson & Hedges, or was it Craven A?). Sir John gave it his all. He rehearsed relentlessly and didn't seem to need to sleep. He and I and Noel sat up till six in the morning at the Randolph Hotel drinking port and doing card tricks. At ten on the morning of the press night, Sir John rang Noel's bedroom.

'Is that Noel Davis? Why aren't you down here?'

'Is that you, Sir John? Where are you? In the foyer?'

'No, you fool. I'm in the fucking theatre where I belong.'

The notices turned out not to be too bad. It didn't *look* great, but it *sounded* well. Indeed, I got into the habit of saying it was possibly, no, it was probably, the best spoken *Joan* since the War. But then I was the producer and to be a producer you have to have gall.

HAPPINESS

'We hold these truths to be sacred and undeniable; that all men are created equal and independent, that from that equal creation they derive rights inherent and inalienable, among which are the preservation of life, and liberty, and the pursuit of happiness.'

Thomas Jefferson's draft for the
American Declaration of Independence

Yes, but what *is* happiness? Michelangelo Antonioni took the line that happiness 'is like the bluebird of Maeterlinck: try to catch it and it loses its colour. It's like trying to hold water in your hands. The more you squeeze it the more it runs away.'

It is elusive, but it is not illusory and I reckon it is more accessible than some would have you believe. At best, it is Abraham Maslow's 'self-actualisation', self-fulfilment and realisation of one's potential; at least, it's a Big Mac and a large portion of fries.

Happiness is looking up rather than looking down, looking out rather than looking in, looking forward rather than looking back. 'Happiness is good health and a bad memory,' said Ingrid Bergman. ('A bad memory is coming into a crowded room full of familiar faces and only having one name spring to mind: Alzheimer,' said Noel Davis. Poor taste, I know, but then I've found that the impeccably politically correct are not a frightfully jolly bunch, well-meaning, but not much fun. They put on a pantomime and call it *Snow Green and the Seven Persons of Restricted Growth*. And I have been told by those in adversity that laughing at it does help. When I met Monja Danischewsky, as he fell back into his chair he said, 'I'm afraid I've got Parkinson's Disease. I'm very much hoping he's got mine.' Monja, as well as producing *Whisky Galore* and writing *Topkapi*, conjured up the Famous Last Words of the Fatted Calf: 'I hear the young master has returned ...')

Happiness is a habit. You can acquire it, like good posture. Okay, on the day the cat's run over and you get the wrong A Level results, it isn't an option, but on an average day for the average fellow, who is neither destitute nor clinically depressed and is living and working in what remains the country with the best climate, the best culture and the best cooked breakfast on the planet earth, happiness is there if you reach out and grab it.

It's a habit that is worth acquiring if only because, like good posture, it makes you look better, it makes you feel better and, whether it's shallow or profound, it's preferable to the alternative. Scoff not at Dale Carnegie, the self-help evangelist and proselytiser of the power of positive thinking: 'Act as if you were already happy and that will tend to make you happy.' It's corny, but it works.

'Happiness,' says Sir Denis Thatcher, 'is a warm summer evening, an open bottle of champagne and the lady in a reasonably contented frame of mind.' Happiness is counting your blessings.

Nine Things That Make Me Happy

1. Food and drink. I will eat absolutely anything and adore it, apart from marzipan, fruit cake, dates and bread and butter pudding. My favourite cuisine is Italian, followed by Indian, Chinese, Turkish and French, in that order. At the end of the working day I love a drink (as a reward rather than a rite) and there are special drinks for special places:

champagne on the Riveria, prosecco in Venice, a daiquiri in Barbados, a raspberry vodka in Moscow, a Manhattan in Manhattan, plonk in the kitchen. I only ever drink beer in one place, a pub whose name I don't know, but where we stop for steak and chips on the drive from Chester to London.

I used to be a nine and a half stone weakling. Now I'm an eleven and a half stone weakling, but the good news is that I have discovered a diet that works. What's more, it's easy to remember. There are just three rules:

a. No bread, rice, pasta or potato.
b. Only eat three times a day.
c. Only eat food traditionally requiring the use of cutlery (i.e. no food with your fingers and no cheating with chopsticks).

Yup, that's it. Three simple rules and you lose 2 lb a week. (Of course you, my boy, don't need to lose an ounce and won't need to – until you are thirty; that's the age it suddenly arrives and stays like an unwelcome lodger. Today, you're a lean, mean fighting machine, but one day your paunch will come and then you'll be glad your old dad handed on the Brandreth Three Rule Diet, the one that's never forgotten and never fails.)

2. Work. Noël Coward used to say that work is more fun than fun. And so it is if you have worked out what work you find fun and found a way to fund it. On the front page of today's *Daily Telegraph* is a report of the farmer's wife from County Galway whose faith paid dividends. She selected the numbers of her lottery ticket by choosing the dates of the Feast of the Assumption of the Virgin Mary, the Immaculate Conception and the Birth of Christ, and has collected the first prize of £2,913,460 as a consequence. She already believed in miracles. On the back page of the same paper is a reproduction of a splendid painting of Viscount Coke, heir to

the Earl of Leicester, surrounded by the team who help him run the ancestral pile at Holkham Hall. The painting is by our friend Andrew Festing, who, when he was still a director of Sotheby's, immortalised in oils my 'longest-ever after-dinner speech' and then decided to exchange the security of the saleroom for the uncertainties of the freelance life. He is now the premier portraitist to the discerning gentry and, from Buckingham Palace (where he is constantly knocking off tip-top likenesses of the monarch and her clan in a bewildering array of outfits and uniforms) to the House of Commons (where one of his best works adorns the Strangers Dining Room and where his next commission is the official portrait of Madam Speaker), they think of him as a first class artist and a very fine fellow. He is both, but I mention him here because he is happy in his work and it is his work that makes him happy. Give him £2,913,460 and he'd say thank you (he has aristo tendencies but he's not a fool) and carry on painting.

3. Sex. Yes, well – er –

4. Sleep. Ah, that's better. I relish my sleep. It's the best kind of oblivion, death without the consequences. I like to sleep and I like to sleep in bed. Indeed, in bed is the only place I ever slept until I became a member of parliament and was introduced to the lunatic practice of the all-night sitting. For a reason that appears to have escaped every other legislature in the world, democracy in the United Kingdom now and again requires debates that go on all night and legislators on hand in case a vote is called. These are the nights when the Library of the House of Commons rumbles to the sound of late middle-aged men snoring as they lie, by the dozen, slumped in green leather armchairs, and the spectacle of elected dossers curled up in sleeping bags in the lower ministerial corridor evokes the sorry sight of shop doorways after dark in the Strand. I knew there would be many

surprises when I arrived at Westminster, but I had not reckoned that sleeping with Harriet Harman would be one of them, and yet, there we were, enduring the Committee Stage of the Finance Bill, dozing fitfully, if not side by side, at least face to face, until we were brought to our senses just in time to vote to abolish the Business Expansion Scheme. As I walked through the lobby at four o'clock one morning with the Foreign Secretary, I asked myself, 'Is there a serious business in the world that would treat its senior management this way?' I was too weary to come up with a coherent answer.

Sleep is good for you. Lack of sleep isn't. Complete lack of sleep will kill you more quickly than complete lack of food. Elephants and dolphins can survive happily with two hours sleep out of every twenty-four and the Emperor Napoleon, who loved his bed ('I would not exchange it for all the thrones in the world'), rarely took more than five hours a night, but the average night's sleep among normal human beings is supposed to be 7 hours and 36 minutes. People in their fifties tend to sleep less than those in their twenties, but people in their sixties get more sleep than at any time since childhood. Men sleep ten minutes more than women (and, to judge from my parliamentary experience of communal slumber, several decibels more loudly), and the difference rises to twenty minutes more in the fifties and fifty minutes more in the seventies. Extroverts of both sexes, and those with low IQs, sleep a little longer than the average.

If you suffer from insomnia, whatever the cause (hypertension, indigestion, a small majority, an inability to reconcile yourself to the prospect of spending twenty to thirty years of your precious life in bed and out for the count), I hope I can help. As a rule, I fall asleep within moments of my head hitting the pillow, but on the odd occasion when it's a struggle to nod off, I don't take a pill, I play a game. It's a simple game in which I make a series of alphabetical lists. You pick a category (characters in

Shakespeare, British Prime Ministers, words that begin and end with the same letter), start at the beginning (Aguecheek, Attlee, aria, Bottom, Balfour, boob, Cassius, Churchill, cardiac, Dogberry, Douglas-Home, dunderhead) and long, long before you get to Walpole or Wilson or the nice question of whether Yorick as a skull can count as a character or whether proper names and exclamations and colloquialisms (like Xerox and wow! and zizz) are permissible, I guarantee you'll be deep in the arms of Morpheus.

5. Words. Of all the extraordinary things that have sprung from our tiny island the greatest is the English language. It has been our most significant export and is perhaps our most undervalued natural resource. We need words for, as the philosopher said, no matter how eloquently a dog may bark he cannot tell you that his parents were poor but honest. To be brought up with English as your parent tongue and, consequently, to have effortless access to the world's richest vocabulary and greatest literature, is a privilege not to be taken for granted. Words bring me happiness. I love to read them. I love to hear them. Michèle and I have just completed listening to thirty-seven hours of our friend Martin Jarvis reading *David Copperfield*. Matchless! Some turn to Mozart to get a buzz. I put on Olivier as Othello addressing the Senate:

> I will a round unvarnished tale deliver
> Of my whole course of love …

I enjoy opera, I enjoy ballet ('A lot of money to see buggers dancing,' said someone), but I *need* words. A good tune is a good tune, but a good lyric is poetry. (A point proven by Alec McCowen the other night when he *recited* Cole Porter's 'You're the Top'. Hutch or Whispering Jack Smith couldn't have sung it better.)

6. Laughter. You know me.

7. My children. You know you. Having you, Benet, and Saethryd and Aphra, has been the most interesting and tiring and delightful and expensive and important and special thing to have happened to me. Having children introduces you to selfless love and changes your life. Sigmund Freud said that 'When we hear the baby laugh it is the loveliest thing that can happen to us'. Mark Twain said that 'a baby is an estimable thing and a bother'. In this instance they both got it spot on, but as to which of them, Freud or Twain, understood the human condition better or contributed more to the sum total of human happiness I wouldn't like to say.

8. My wife. You know her. She's your mother. I was there so I know it's true. I have always tried to avoid commenting on other people's marriages, because I'm not sure I understand my own. I have a feeling that talking about how good it is may be like tempting providence or being featured in *Hello!* I'm just keeping my head down, my stomach in and my fingers crossed.

9. My life. None of us can be happy all the time, but it would be a poor show for someone who has had the privileges and pleasures heaped onto them that I have had, ever seriously to complain about anything. In return for all the good things I do feel a certain obligation to be cheerful.

Cecil Parkinson was 'In the Psychiatrist's Chair' on the radio yesterday morning and acknowledged that, until the trauma of the Sara Keays affair, he had not been given to much introspection or critical self-examination. Dr Anthony Clare remarked that it was not unusual for it to take a major trauma to stop a person and make them think. Not long ago I got up feeling at my happiest, stepped out of the front door, sensed summer in the air and a spring in my heel. The boiled egg at breakfast had been perfect, the newsprint didn't come off on my hand, an empty bus arrived as I reached the bus stop. As I trundled down the stairs to the tube, my train came rollicking into the platform. On I hopped, off it went and when I reached my destination the doors opened immediately in front of the very Exit I needed. I thought, 'Yes, this is my lucky day,' went through the Exit, turned sharp right and walked, slap, bang, wollop straight into a brick wall. Happiness is keeping happiness in check.

JUMPERS

'Do not despair – many are happy much of the time; more eat than
starve, more are healthy than sick, more curable than dying; not so
many dying as dead; and one of the thieves was saved. Hell's bells
and all's well – half the world is at peace with itself, and so is the
other half; vast areas are unpolluted; millions of children grow up
without suffering deprivation, and millions, while deprived, grow
up without suffering cruelties, and millions, while deprived and
cruelly treated, none the less grow up. No laughter is sad and many
tears are joyful.'

Tom Stoppard, *Jumpers*

Tom Stoppard has an alarmingly brilliant way with words. I
warm to his wit and his humanity; I envy his intelligence and
capacity for dazzling linguistic pyrotechnics. A few years
ago, when I was struggling to put on a show at the
Cambridge Festival based on the life and works of A A Milne
(with charming music by Julian Slade, and Aled Jones
inspirationally cast as Christopher Robin), I dreamt of
Stoppard, in the same city, effortlessly running up an opera
of Stephen Hawking's *A Brief History of Time*. Each to his
own. Tom Stoppard's *Jumpers* is a work of genius. My
jumpers, by contrast, a chance exercise in 'branding'.

Don't get me wrong. I never knock my happy association
with colourful knitwear. I just keep it in perspective. I no
longer keep it in the cupboard, because since giving up
television to go into politics I have thrown away the

mothballs and given away the jumpers – hundreds of them, in every shape and size, in every colour of the rainbow. I am pleased to say they have helped raise some useful sums for some worthy causes. Jeffrey Archer was the under-bidder for the last one I auctioned. It went for £1,000. The Duke of Westminster paid £1,100 for his.

In the year Tom Stoppard wrote *Jumpers*, I founded the National Scrabble Championships. Michèle and I were living in a flat in Muswell Hill and I placed a small ad in the Personal Column of *The Times* inviting anyone interested in taking part to write to me there. Within days hundreds of letters had arrived, including one from the official PR people for Scrabble saying 'How dare you?' It was a relief to hear from them because I hadn't realised that my innocuous ad would unleash such an avalanche of correspondence from demented word-buffs across the land. We got together, we became friends and we successfully established an annual event that has stood the test of time. Thousands now take part in the National Scrabble Championships, there's a world championship, Scrabble clubs in every corner of the earth, Scrabble T-shirts, Scrabble mugs, Scrabble on TV. There's even a Scrabble Puzzles magazine, of which I am proud to be the founding editor-in-chief.

In 1974, when Tom Stoppard won the *Evening Standard* Award for *Travesties*, a young lady turned up at the finals of the National Scrabble Championships with a present for me: a bright yellow jumper with emblazoned on the chest a replica of a Scrabble board with interlocking tiles carrying the message: GYLES BRANDRETH LOVES SCRABBLE. I donned the garment. Its appearance on the platform provoked a gratifying smattering of applause. And so the jumper man was born.

Appearance counts. I learnt that from Renée Houston when I was making one of my very first panel game appearances and she was making one of her last. It was a radio programme, recorded in front of a live audience ('live'

does them more than justice) at the Playhouse Theatre in
Northumberland Avenue. Miss Houston and I were standing
together in the wings and moments before we were due on
stage, she opened her handbag, rummaged about and
produced a roll of Sellotape.

'This has to be done at the last minute. It only holds for
about half an hour.'

She handed me the Sellotape and with both hands scooped
up her jowls and double chin and pulled the skin firmly
towards the back of her neck.

'Now,' she instructed, 'tear off a strip of tape and stick me
down.'

She had folded over a hefty handful of skin which she
pressed into the nape of her neck while I fixed it in place with
strips of Sellotape. From the rear it looked horrendous. From
the front, and as she took the stage she took it sideways so
that's all they saw, it looked more than presentable.

I think Stoppard was completing *Dirty Linen* when I first
visited Barbara Cartland at Camfield Place, near Hatfield. I
think she was just completing *The Prude and the Prodigal* (or
was it *The Goddess and the Gaiety Girl*?). Anyway, she
looked a picture, a mature sugar plum fairy decked from
neck to calf in a sparkling confection of pink tulle. 'She looks
like a Christmas tree,' muttered the sound engineer who was
with me. 'And don't we all love Christmas?' trilled Miss
Cartland as she led us into the drawing room where she sat
bolt upright in a high-backed armchair and was lit by her
own special theatrical lamps that successfully accentuated
her natural rosy hue.

'I'm afraid it's only a radio interview,' I ventured.

'I know, my dear, but I always like to look my best. It's
simply a matter of courtesy.'

Miss Cartland was the personification of *politesse* – and
professionalism. Through the interview she twinkled and
sparkled and gurgled (and plugged her books and her record
and her honey), and on the stroke of four marched us to the

dining room for a proper tea (including mouth-melting meringues). She left us briefly at one stage during the afternoon and, as we departed, we discovered why. Each member of the crew was presented with one of her books, personally inscribed, and individually wrapped up with pink ribbon. 'A little souvenir, lest you forget ...'

Lest we forget! Love her or loathe her, Miss Cartland, the vitamin virgin, the Liberace of literature, the queen of romance, once encountered, is not likely to be forgotten. Her branding is strong, her niche market carefully carved out, her success deserved and sustained. Barbara Cartland had the colour pink. Harry Corbett had Sooty. Bernie Winters had Snorbitz. Eric had Ernie. And I had jumpers. As Clive James said to me, 'Some people have to pull an act together. All you have to do is pull on a jersey.'

I had jerseys and guernseys and tank-tops and cardies. I had knitwear for every occasion. Jumpers for Christmas, jumpers for Easter, a jumper with a pancake on it for Shrove Tuesday; jumpers to promote products, jumpers to support causes (the one backing the campaign to halt the imposition of VAT on books was misinterpreted: the jumper said 'DON'T TAX READING' and the citizens of Reading took it to mean them); spooky jumpers for Hallowe'en, happy jumpers for the holidays; even, at TV-am, a sombre jumper to be slipped into in the event that the death of the Queen Mother had to be announced while we were on air. (It was kept in a special filing cabinet 'just in case'.) My favourites were made for me by George Hostler and featured teddy bears, cats of all kinds and exotic birds. ('Isn't that a parakeet?' asked Anne Diamond on air one morning. 'Don't be silly, Anne,' said Katie Boyle who was sharing the sofa. 'You must have seen a cockatoo before now.')

The essence of a good trademark is that it is good for trade. The jumpers were that. They didn't bring me fame and fortune (I am only slightly well-known and not nearly as well-off as I aimed to be, dammit), but in the amorphous nomad's land of game shows and on the lost horizon of breakfast TV they gave me a certain 'definition', which I acknowledge with gratitude. They also led to me becoming a director of a chain of thirty-nine wool shops and earning a tasty packet promoting the tastiness of packets of Bird's Eye potato waffles.

Research shows that 83% of what people recall from television is what they see, not what they hear. Even now, more than three years after I last appeared on the box in a memorable woollie, invariably the first thing I am asked by a stranger who 'knows the face, but ... ' is 'Who makes your jumpers?' Rather to my surprise, during the recent Committee Stage of the Railways Bill, John Prescott, Labour's Transport spokesman (whose mother happens to be a valued constituent of mine), snorted 'Woolly jumper!' at me derisively. I had to point out to him that the joy of a woolly jumper is that you can take it off at will, while the penalty of a woolly mind is that you are lumbered with it for life. (I wonder if Prescott's own apparent indifference to his personal appearance is self-conscious? 'An essentially private man who wished his total indifference to public notice to be universally recognised,' *Travesties*, Act 1.) Appearances count. I imagine one of the reasons that Dr John Cunningham became Labour's Shadow Foreign Secretary is that he looks the part.

My jumpers never conquered America. In 1988 I had hopes that they might. I was invited to be a guest on *The Late Show*, Fox TV's answer to Johnny Carson's *Tonight Show* and, at that time, apparently rivalling it in terms of network audience. I went because I wanted to use the exposure to promote an important pet project, the Royal Britain exhibition at the Barbican, a multi-media experience that aimed to bring a thousand years of royal history to life and nine hundred thousand visitors a year to the Barbican. Unfortunately, we were attracting a quarter that number and needed all the help we could get. Along with my distinctive

Royal Britain jumper, I packed King Canute's crown and a desperately heavy fur-trimmed cape. Television is a visual medium and I was determined to make an impact.

I flew first class to LA (the only advantage is that you feel safer; disconcertingly the folk travelling steerage arrive at exactly the same time as you do) where a smoked-glass stretch limo was waiting to take me to my hotel where a second, even stretchier stretch limo (complete with cocktail cabinet and colour TV) was waiting to purr me to the studio. We recorded 'as live' at seven for transmission across the nation at 11.00 pm. Ensconced in my dressing room (onto the door of which my name had been *painted*) I began to run through the anecdotes about Canute and King Arthur and the other 'colourful kings and queens whose human story we are bringing to life in a unique right-royal roller-coaster ride through history'.

The show's host put his head around the door: 'Great to meet you, Guy. I just love your accent.' I hadn't spoken yet. 'You're in the last quarter of the show. We keep the best till last! We've got a big, big audience tuning in to catch you tonight!'

Before I could say hello, good evening or thank you for the welcome, he'd gone. I was whisked to make-up, provided with an instant Californian tan, and returned to my room where, secretly, I donned my jumper, crown and cape. The producer had vetoed the costume, but I was ready to defy her. As I ran through my mental checklist of Royal Britain's most glorious features – the tableaux of Richard the Lionheart at the Crusades, the animatronic of Elizabeth addressing the troops at Tilbury, the Christmas scene with Victoria and Albert – the monitor sprang to life, the opening credits began to roll, the studio audience burst into frenetic applause and mine host slid down the banister onto the set as his devotees squealed their adoration and delight. 'And on tonight's show,' he cooed, 'all the way from London, England, we'll have Guy Brandon, who is going to lift the

veil on Bucking-ham Palace and dish the dirt on those
raunchy royals. If you're watching, Fergie, watch out!' I trust
the Duchess of York had better things to do that evening. I
certainly felt I had, but I could see no way out of it. As my
sinking heart sunk lower, on the monitor I could see our host
introducing the first guest, who looked like Walter Matthau
(if only!) but turned out to be a psychic, 'a medium rare'
quipped our host, who at the crackle of a contract could
make instant contact with the world beyond. To order he
locked himself into a trance and proceeded to bring
individual messages to members of the studio audience who
gasped and cheered and, in the case of one widow, wept
copiously as word reached her that her late husband was
ready to forgive her.

The medium switched out of his trance just in time for the
commercial break. The floor manager appeared at my
dressing room. 'He's such a sensation, we're keeping him on
a tad longer. You're down to seven minutes, but don't worry,
Guy, it's a big audience and they're tuning in to catch *you*.'
Hadn't I heard that somewhere before? She took me by the
hand and led me along a series of corridors to the studio. I
stood in darkness at the edge of the set and watched and
waited as the medium with the messages enjoyed his night of
triumph. With three minutes of air-time left to run, I heard
our host declare: 'And now, after that shattering, truly
shattering experience, on a night to remember, I think you'll
agree ladies and gentlemen this has been A Night to
Remember!' – the moist-eyed audience clapped and cheered,
'Before we go let's look East to England and let's get at the
truth. We're going to tear back the curtains at Bucking-ham
Palace and to help us here's the man who knows *all* the royal
secrets, Guy Branson!' And on stumbled King Canute.

Our host had not been expecting the crown and cape, but
he took them in his stride, with style, going down on one
knee and saying, 'Arise, Sir Guy!' as I flopped onto the studio
sofa.

'We've only got sixty seconds, Guy, so let's get down to the nitty-gritty. Is it true that Chuck and Di don't do it any more?'

'I – er – I don't really know,' I countered lamely, 'but I can tell you that at Royal Britain at the Barbican you get a right-royal roller-coaster of kings and queens, from the reign of Edgar ...'

And that was it. The music played, the credits rolled, our host was up, off and away to embrace the medium and book him for a return engagement. The limo that took me back to my hotel was hardly stretched at all.

I didn't bother turning on the television till 11.57 pm – I couldn't face the medium's triumph twice in one night. I know envy is corrosive, but there you are. As it turned out, three minutes to midnight was still too early. President Reagan was addressing the Republican Convention that night and *The Late Show* was rescheduled. I finally hit the screen a little before two in the morning. It was not an impressive sight, but it was certainly a man wearing a crown and a cape and, under the cape, if you looked very closely you could just about read 'OYAL BRI'.

In London it was six o'clock and Tom Stoppard had just completed the first draft of *Arcadia*.

KINDRED SPIRITS

'What great cause is he identified with?'
'He's identified ... with the great cause of cheering us all up.'
Last words of *The Card* by Arnold Bennett

Before I discovered Stoppard, Jean-Paul Sartre was my hero. By the age of sixteen I had read all his published plays (in the little *Livre de Poche* editions that still smell so good after all these years), not necessarily understanding much (indeed I now suspect I may have got entirely the wrong end of the stick because I found them *exhilarating* which may not be the effect they are intended to have), but relishing the language and flattering myself that I was *au courant* with the mind and *oeuvre* of the father of existentialism.

One night in the summer of 1962 I set out to meet my hero. I remember the occasion with such clarity because it came at the end of the most traumatic ten days of my life, ten days in which I had visited ten different European countries in the lone company of someone I felt indifferent towards at the beginning of the expedition and heartily loathed by the end.

My cousin Johnnie was eighteen, Canadian, blond, bull-necked but good-looking in a dead-behind-the-eyes sort of way. He was over to 'do Europe' and my parents had the bright idea that Johnnie and I might 'do' it together. They loaned us the family car and the plan was that Johnnie would drive and I would navigate as we poodled round the Continent, sight-seeing by day and camping by night. However, once we hit the open road it became clear that Johnnie was not interested so much in viewing sites as in collecting countries. 'Doing Europe' to Johnnie meant amassing stamps in his passport. On the first day we traversed France. We started in Caen and ended up in Carcassonne, having taken in Le Mans, Tours, Limoges and Toulouse en route. We stopped for nothing, except petrol and milk. The Ford Consul guzzled petrol and Johnnie guzzled milk. He drank as he drove, ruthlessly, tearing open the milk carton with his teeth, slurping down the contents noisily and then flinging the empty carton out onto the road. He kept his window permanently open which, given the speed at which we were travelling, meant we had to shout at one another to be heard. On the second day we touched base with Andorra, spent an hour in Spain and made Marseilles by nightfall.

'Let's hit the red light district,' said Johnnie with a macho chuckle.

'I have no idea where it is,' I said primly, 'it isn't marked on the map.'

'It'll be round the docks,' said Johnnie with a knowing leer. We followed the signs to the port and found our way to a dark and dreary square where Johnnie's second sense told him we would see some action. We drove round and round the deserted square with Johnnie peering up at the shuttered windows hoping to catch a glimpse of one of the 'ladies of the night'. When none appeared, Johnnie sounded the horn furiously and we sped off towards Monte Carlo.

Whenever we arrived in a new country Johnnie would buy a batch of postcards (never of views, always of buxom bathing beauties either sitting on or playing with beach balls) to mail to his galaxy of girlfriends back home. I do not recall us visiting one church or monument or gallery, but in each territory we visited Johnnie enquired, 'Where's Hitler's bunker? It would be good to see one of Hitler's bunkers. Do you think he had one around here?'

When we reached Italy I decided to move from the front seat to the back. I was finding my companion's company so difficult to endure that I could no longer bear to look at him. To pass the time as we raced through Switzerland, Austria and Germany towards Holland and Belgium, we played a word game called Donkey. It is a spelling game where the players take it in turn to add a letter and build a word, the loser being the player who is forced to complete a word. We played hundreds, possibly thousands, of games as we roared from autostrada to autobahn and, because I couldn't bear to let my cousin win, I cheated. Sitting behind the driver, out of his eyeline, I could use a dictionary.

After ten days we had run out of countries – and cash – and conversation – and found ourselves back in Caen. Our custom was to park off the main road and to sleep either just by the car or in it. On this particular night Johnnie was in his sleeping bag on the verge and I was stretched out on the back seat with my feet sticking out of the window. (There was a painful ridge behind my ankles most mornings.) It wasn't late, but it was getting too dark to finish *Les Mains Sales*, and we were tired and bored. I had covered my face with my jacket and was busy thinking unkind thoughts about my Canadian kith and kin when I sensed someone scratching the ball of my foot. I sat up and was confronted by an amiable bearded grin at the window.

'Sorry to trouble you,' the fellow said, in impeccable English, 'but I need to get to Deauville and I wondered if you could give me a lift.'

He told us he was Dutch, and a poet, and in his apartment in Utrecht had a gigantic circular bed that could sleep four women comfortably. 'Sex between two people is beautiful ... between five, it's a sensation!' Johnnie wanted to hear more – and could if we would give Max a ride to Deauville.

'Why Deauville?'

'I'm meeting up with Jean-Paul Sartre. We have some things we need to talk about.'

The bar where Max and Sartre were set to have their *rendez-vous* was in the centre of Deauville; we found it without difficulty and arrived around midnight. The bar was crowded, but with people who looked more like tourists than existentialists. 'It seems Jean-Paul has failed to show,' said Max, with a shrug. 'Typical. Will you have a drink?'

Johnnie asked for a Scotch. Never having drunk spirits before, I said I'd have the same. We took our drinks onto the verandah, above the rocks leading down to the sea, and stood looking out over the bay. Max and Johnnie talked about their sex lives. I sniffed at the whisky and, under the cover of darkness, poured my Scotch on the rocks and concluded that Sartre had been right in *Huis Clos*: 'Hell is other people.'

Hugh Kingsmill said, 'Friends are God's apology for relations.' I happen to like my immediate family, my mother, brother and sisters, very much. I have even learnt to like Johnnie, who turns out now to be cultured, good-humoured and in charge of much of Canada's prison service. Only recently did it dawn on me that I was the guilty party: a bumptious, supremely self-centred and intolerant child. The consolation of growing older is that you become less self-centred; the danger is that you become more intolerant.

The son of Sir Walter Raleigh (no, not that one, Sir Walter A Raleigh, who became first Professor of English Literature at Oxford in 1904) published a posthumous collection of his father's lighter writings under the endearing title, *Laughter from a Cloud*. It contains a little verse that regularly springs to mind when emerging from a party to which one should never have accepted an invitation in the first place:

> I wish I loved the Human Race;
> I wish I loved its silly face;
> I wish I liked the way it walks;

> I wish I liked the way it talks;
> And when I'm introduced to one
> I wish I thought *What Jolly Fun*!

I am getting better with new people. I don't believe I am trying harder; I am just hanging looser. (I am still not as tolerant with the tipsy as I might be. The problem is not so much their inebriation as my sobriety. I go to too many functions where I am the speaker: as my motto is 'Don't drink and drivel', and as you probably need to drink quite heavily to listen to me, by the time 'the formal part of the proceedings have been concluded' I find myself standing in the bar surrounded by happy folk who are getting louder and closer all the time. The loudest and the closest have a tendency to spray you with remnants of their supper. (My boy, when I grow old will you ensure that, if I go out, I go out with a clean jacket, teeth that fit and ears and nostrils that don't immediately bring the Forest of Arden to mind?)

Sometimes, when we are about to enter a room filled with unfamiliar faces, Michèle will look at my grouchy countenance and say, 'How would Jeremy Hanley face this?' With a smile is the answer. Jeremy, son of Jimmy Hanley and Dinah Sheridan, now Armed Forces Minister, formerly a junior minister in Northern Ireland, is always bonhomous. Whether it is a gift or a skill, it is certainly a strength, and one he deploys to wonderful effect. High or low, shattered or merely exhausted, Jeremy is always amiable, open and apparently interested in you and what you have to say and offer. He has a cheerfulness that is cheering, a generosity of spirit that is very comfortable to be with. (Actually, he is generous to a fault. On my first day at the Commons he entertained Michèle and me to lunch followed by a guided tour. When, three days later, on *Wogan* I recycled the best of his *bon mots* he went out of his way to say 'Well done!')

I am advised that to the Chinese we Europeans all look the same and that the way we smell is not to their taste.

Incredible as it may seem, my boy, there will be people who regard you and me as crashing bores. That's just the way things are. I don't advise you to seek out bores for the good of your soul, but when you meet them try the Hanley approach: be genial, be generous.

Derek Nimmo is one of London's most genial and generous hosts – his must be the only household in Earl's Court where, when you go to dinner, there are not just staff, but liveried footmen waiting at table – and he shares this capacity (Martin Jarvis has it too) for appearing at ease with all-comers, be they dukes or dustmen (he is particularly interested in dustmen who were dukes: his own chauffeur is a scion of the aristocracy). Derek has the gift of curiosity; he travels the world, in style, is interested in everything that happens outside himself and seems the happier for it.

Our mutual friend Kenneth Williams was all too concerned with what was happening inside himself (from his bowels to his soul) and certainly the unhappier for it. I got to know Kenneth quite well over the last ten years of his life and, in the hundreds of hours and scores of meals we shared, he never once inflicted on me the waspish side of his nature. He could be sweet and sour, but when he came to our house was only sweet. Sure, he was outrageous, wickedly funny, and often wicked simply to be funny. He would say terrible things about people, dreadful, hurtful, calumnious things, without necessarily meaning them, or, if meaning them, meaning them for the moment, or, if really meaning them, not meaning them to hurt. He would go as far as he needed – and frequently far beyond – to create an effect, to provoke a reaction, if necessary of shock, preferably of hysteria. (One evening after dinner, when he already had the crowded table in a roar, he got to his feet, spun round, dropped his trousers and cried, 'Look, look! The bum – it's hanging down in pleats!') He made me laugh a lot. With his work on radio (particularly), on television and in the *Carry Ons* he made us all laugh a lot. In a way I am sorry that his diaries are now in print, albeit admirably edited, because seeing some of the harsh, intolerant, occasionally intolerable, things he has to say may deceive those who did not know him well. Reading the diaries you only get half of Kenneth: he kept the worst for himself and shared the best with others.

We worked on his three books together and I dipped into his diaries when he was still alive. He did not want them published. 'Some sides of my character aren't presentable' was his line. He was aware of his own shortcomings and exaggerated them. He knew that when he was angry with himself, and let it show, it spoiled his work. He recognised that his outlandish behaviour distanced some who wanted to be better friends. One of his oldest chums was the film director, John Schlesinger, who had been with Kenneth, and Stanley Baxter and Peter Nichols, in Combined Services Entertainments in the Far East in the 1940s, putting on those concert parties so brilliantly memorialised in Nichols's *Privates on Parade*. John hadn't seen Kenneth for some years, so we invited them for supper. John was apprehensive, fearing an evening of self-centred queeniness: in the event Kenneth was on his best behaviour, sweet, slightly sentimental, affectionate, fun. John suggested a re-match at his house. It didn't work: Kenneth was at his worst, he started loud and funny and, as the evening wore on, got louder and less funny. The problem, I guess, was that Alan Bennett had joined the party, and was so quiet and so droll that Kenneth couldn't cope with the competition, and couldn't bear himself for seeing it as competition. His very gifts would add to his self-loathing. 'Most good talkers, when they have run down, are miserable,' said Cyril Connolly, 'they know that they have betrayed themselves, that they have taken material which should have a life of its own to dispense it in noises upon the air.'

When Kenneth killed himself, I was not altogether surprised – he had told me that his father committed suicide – but I was much saddened. He was a consummate performer, a considerable raconteur and a gentler, more generous friend than his diaries might lead you to believe. He was particularly kind at the time my father died and sent me a note urging me to bear up and remember Nietzsche's advice: 'To endure is all'. He also introduced me to Hilaire Belloc's *Dedicatory Ode*:

> From quiet homes and first beginning,
> Out to the undiscovered ends,
> There's nothing worth the wear of winning,
> But laughter and the love of friends.

LUST

'The expense of spirit in a waste of shame.'
William Shakespeare

Kenneth Williams liked a filthy story, and he particularly liked a filthy story well told. On 21 June 1985 he came to dinner at our house on Campden Hill when Roddy Llewellyn was another of the guests. Kenneth noted in his diary:

'Roddy told a story about a man going into the home of two spinsters to view a Ming vase & seeing a french letter lying on the piano stool. The old lady explained "We found it lying in the grass on the common & it said *Place on organ to avoid infection* and we haven't got an organ so we put it on the piano & do you know we've neither of us had *any colds* this year!" He's one of the few people I've ever come upon who knows how to tell a story.'

Kenneth would have enjoyed the story Noel told at lunch on Sunday. In passing, you had mentioned the Brigade of Gurkhas, and Noel, with his extraordinary capacity for finding a tale for every subject, immediately launched into the saga of the flighty lady at the military cocktail party who was introduced to a Colonel in the Gurkhas and burst out, 'Oh, goodness, Colonel, you've quite taken me aback. You're *white*. I thought all you Gurkhas were black.' 'No, no,' said the Colonel, 'only our privates are black.' 'Oh,' gasped the lady, 'how thrilling!'

That is, of course, an unacceptable story at a variety of levels, but having been on the northern club circuit with Bernard Manning I have heard worse, much worse. In the late seventies and early eighties I found I was being booked as an after-dinner speaker at sportsmen's dinners and men-only events where something blue (rather than True Blue) might have been expected, but, happily, wasn't mandatory. If you were funny you didn't have to be filthy. I never told dirty stories, nor used bad language, and seemed to get away with it. At a stag dinner you can. On a Friday night at the Pied Piper Club, Wigan, when you've been billed as the warm-up for Bernard Manning, it isn't so easy. My act that night went neither well nor badly: it went unnoticed. As soon as they saw me the management must have sensed that I was not quite what they (or their punters) were expecting and decided that, during my routine, soft music would continue to play and I would share the stage with a couple of topless go-go dancers.

I shared a dressing room, such as it was, with the stripper, a genial lady (a mother of three, it transpired), who, while I was pulling on my jumper was pulling off hers. She was being paid more than me and gave more too. As she slapped on the body make-up and hummed a medley of Abba hits, I sat in the corner pretending to do *The Times* crossword, affecting the nonchalance of an old trooper thoroughly accustomed to sharing a dressing room the size of a shoe box with Lancashire's answer to Gypsy Rose Lee. She was friendly and seemed eager to chat, and when I glanced up from Three Across and caught her eye I tried to make sure it was her eye I caught.

'I've been doing this for years,' she confided. 'Whatever they say it is an art, you know.'

'I'm sure,' I replied, brow furrowed, nose buried in Seven Down.

'When I started we used to be called "erotic dancers". Didn't use to have to do the whole strip then.'

'No indeed,' I muttered, biting my pencil as she sorted out the left tassle.

'Eh, luv,' she said advancing upon me, 'would you help sequin me bum?'

Laying aside my paper and thinking 'we artistes must stick together,' I did as I was asked and proceeded to apply the Pritt Stick to her rear-end, followed by a heavy sprinkling of sequins.

'They love to see your cheeks sparkle,' she said with gusto and a rather touching professional pride. 'It drives 'em wild.'

Truth to tell, her performance was greeted with respectful silence followed by muted applause. Bernard Manning, mercifully clothed and mercilessly lewd, was what they wanted and, when he had given them forty minutes of sure-fire filth, they roared for more.

About a month later I found myself booked to appear at a men-only dinner at Leicester University. There were just two speakers: myself and Dr Rachel Jenkins (a pseudonym, of course), Reader in Mathematics at Swansea. I spoke my piece and it went well enough, though I was apprehensive as to the ride Dr Jenkins might get as the audience was fairly merry and seemed to be in a mood for ribaldry rather than a learned discourse on higher mathematics. I need not have worried. When her turn came, Dr Jenkins rose to her feet and began to deliver her address with singular authority. For the first two or three minutes all went well, then a loutish voice called from the back, 'Get 'em off, darlin'!' Suddenly there was no holding them. From around the hall the cries came, 'Show us what you've got, doctor! Give us a thrill, love! Go on, get 'em off, off, OFF!' This was too much for Dr Jenkins. She clambered onto her chair, and then onto the table in front of her, and then – believe it or not, but I was there and *it is true* – took off every stitch of clothing before leaving the hall to the most tumultuous standing ovation I have been privileged to hear.

I had an over-exposure to naked flesh at a comparatively early age thanks to the seventh Earl of Longford. I was 23 and a year or so out of Oxford and he was 66 and a year or so out of the Cabinet when he telephoned to invite me to join the group he was establishing to investigate 'the whole question of pornography'. Flatteringly, he told me he wanted me on board because I was 'so perceptive' and the only other youthful member of the team so far was Cliff Richard. Foolishly, I believed him. (My boy, beware of flatterers. Don't ask yourself if what they are telling you is true; ask yourself *why* they are telling it to you at all.)

Michèle predicted it would end in tears. 'What do you know about pornography anyway?'

'Probably as much as Lord Longford,' I said.

'Exactly.'

When the group met for the first time it became immediately apparent that it was a gathering of the great and the all-too-good and that, however much Frank Longford might trumpet the 'independence and open-mindedness' of his hand-picked colleagues, it seemed unlikely from the outset that our report would come out in favour of pornography. Our number included an archbishop, two bishops, a rabbi, judges, lawyers, medics, industrialists, Malcolm Muggeridge, Peregrine Worsthorne and, epitomising the youth culture of the time, Cliff and me. Lord Longford set the tone by welcoming us all to the 'crusade' and explaining that he had worked with Sir William Beveridge on the Beveridge Report that established the welfare state as we know it and he trusted our work would prove as significant.

For over a year we gathered 'evidence', from the police, from the medical profession, from broadcasters, from the pornographers themselves. Mostly the witnesses came to see us in the rooms where we met at London University. Occasionally we would allow ourselves an investigative field trip. Peregrine Worsthorne returned from one to report that Soho was awash with men in dirty raincoats claiming to be Lord Longford's research assistants.

I remember a particularly happy lunch at the Garrick Club with Lord L and Alexander Walker, then, as now, film critic of the London *Evening Standard*. Alexander, with his Cannes tan very much in evidence, gave us a crisp run-down on the current cinema scene and warned us that even more explicit screen sex and violence were on their way. Despite these grim tidings Frank remained in mellow mood. The day before he had been to Windsor for his installation as one of Her Majesty's Knights of the Garter. Alexander seemed surprised to see the eccentric earl, whom he may have perceived as an ascetic as well as a puritan, tucking into the Club Beaune with such relish. 'I enjoy wine,' said Frank, beaming, 'and sex, very much so. I have had eight children, you know, and I regularly swim in the nude.'

One evening he suggested I join him and a couple of the female members of our band for an outing to the cinema. We met for supper in the Ladies Annexe at the Athenaeum and decided we would hunt in pairs. His Lordship was anxious to take his companion to see Mike Nichols's new release, *Catch-22*.

'Does that count as pornography, Frank?' I asked.

'From what I've heard it does.'

'But isn't it a sort of black comedy?'

'We shall see.'

Frank and his lady settled on *Catch-22*, while I and mine (a recently qualified nurse who had been brought on board to beef up the youth element of the group) plumped for more predictable fare: a double-bill of *Anybody's Body* and *Collective Marriage*.

The highlight of our year's work was the charabanc outing to Copenhagen. Others tried to dissuade Frank from going, fearing he would lay himself open to ridicule, but he was determined. 'We need to know the worst,' he declared. 'Nobody is going to be able to say that our researches haven't been thorough.' (The unkind also said he would relish the prospect of the publicity, whether favourable or

not. They were the ones who told the story of him rushing
into Hatchards in Piccadilly one day, demanding to see the
manager. 'Why haven't you got a display of my new book in
the window?' 'What's the title?' asked the manager.
'*Humility*,' said Frank.)

Six of our team were selected for the three-day excursion
to Denmark. I sat next to Frank on the flight out and he read
the Bible all the way. He seemed truly an innocent abroad,
and his innocence did not appear self-conscious or contrived.
When, at our first port of call, he was introduced to a totally
naked young woman, I don't believe he noticed. He certainly
didn't bat an eyelid. There was something endearingly
other-worldly about him. We had lunch together in the
Tivoli Gardens and, after the meal, he inadvertently put on
my jacket instead of his own. Despite the fact that the sleeves
only reached his elbows he didn't seem to notice.

The press attention he could not fail to notice. We were at
the centre of an extraordinary caravanserai of Fleet Street
hacks and photographers who were ready to send us up
rotten at every opportunity – and we gave them plenty. We
met with officials from the Ministry of Justice who appeared
perplexed that so distinguished a British parliamentarian (a
Labour Minister in the forties, fifties and sixties) should be
taking such an interest in the subject: their view was that
deregulation had led to a fall in domestic consumption of
pornography, a view confirmed by the 'porn magnate' we
met who maintained that his business was almost entirely
export and would collapse if Germany, Japan and the United
Kingdom relaxed their own anti-porn laws. A benevolent
and bearded psychologist, Berl Kutshinsky, assured us that a
more open attitude to sex would lead to a reduction in sex
crimes and adduced as evidence the fact that in Denmark,
since liberalisation, sex crimes registered by the police had
dropped from 4364 in 1963 to 2819 in 1969.

The press covered our every movement (and lack of
movement – a photographer was stationed in the hotel

corridor between my room and that of the Committee's young female researcher in the vain hope of catching nocturnal perambulations) and gleefully reported each close encounter of the lurid kind. When night fell and we turned out for the 'live sex shows' the reptiles came into their own. Lord L couldn't stomach the entertainment he had been booked in to see and, after not many minutes, walked out. The club's manager was bewildered and pursued him into the street, pleading, 'But you haven't seen the intercourse.' With an instinctive ear for the telling sound-bite, Lord Longford replied that he had 'seen enough for science and more than enough for pleasure', and stomped back to the hotel. I think he might also have seen the *News of the World* photographer lurking. At the point Frank made his excuses and left, the star of the show, stark naked, whip in hand, had just left the small stage and was mingling with the crowd, plonking herself down on the welcoming laps of assorted members of the audience. Had she landed in Lord Longford's lap ... well, click, flash and around the world in eighty minutes would have gone pictures of the elderly English milord with the naked Danish dolly on his noble knee.

The press coverage, as it was, was bad enough. Lord Porn, as he was known generally now by public and cartoonists alike, became a substantial figure of fun, and, such as it was, the Committee's currency was further devalued. I am ashamed to admit that I joined in the gentle lampooning myself, bowing out of the Committee and producing a lightly satirical account of our proceedings for the magazine *Nova*. I even took to giving talks on my experiences with Lord Longford amid the alien porn. My lecture was entitled 'Pornography in Perspective'. One ladies' luncheon club secretary enquired, 'Do you bring slides?'

The Longford Committee's Report, carrying forty-seven signatures and running to 437 pages of text, with seventy-five pages of appendices, was published in September 1972. It defined pornography as 'that which exploits and dehumanizes sex, so that human beings are treated as things, and women in particular as sex objects'. It quarrelled with the present definition of obscenity (that which has a 'tendency to deprave and corrupt') and suggested instead 'any publication or performance which causes outrage to the majority of people'. The report proposed that purveyors of 'hard porn' be prosecuted without qualification and those of 'soft porn' if they displayed their wares publicly. It urged legal sanctions to deter those who exploited performers taking part in pornographic productions, and over all, and above all, it urged a raising of moral standards through stricter controls of the media.

Twenty years after the event, I would quarrel still with some of the Report's methodology, with several of its conclusions, with the practicality of many of its proposed solutions, but looking back on it now I reckon Lord Longford had the right instinct. Alexander Walker was right too: there was more sex and violence still to come. In the cinema, on the box, in the tabloids, material appears today that would have been unthinkable a generation ago. When I was a boy the Sunday evening classic serial on BBC television was RD Blackmore's *Lorna Doone*. This year it is DH Lawrence's *Lady Chatterley's Lover*.

At the first meeting of the Longford Group's television sub-committee, Malcolm Muggeridge reminded us of the BBC's statement of intent, inscribed on the wall in the entrance to Broadcasting House: 'This temple of the arts and muses is dedicated to Almighty God by the first governors in the year 1931, Sir John Reith being Director-General. It is their prayer that good seed sown may bring forth a good harvest, that all things hostile to peace or purity may be banished from this house, and that the people, inclining their ears to whatsoever things are beautiful and honest and of good report, may tread the paths of wisdom and righteousness.'

Has dear old Auntie lost her way?

MONEY

'I'm told a fool and his money are soon parted. What I want to
know is how they got together in the first place.'

Cyril Fletcher

When I was presenting *Son et Lumière*, Cyril Fletcher
appeared in each production. You don't remember Cyril?
Pity. He was rather stylish. Still is, for that matter. He is
eighty now, he's hung up his panto frocks (what a Mother
Goose!), he's put away his 'Odd Odes' (his trademark was
comic verse rather than comic jumpers), and lives in happy
retirement with his beautiful garden and even more beautiful
wife, Betty Astell, on the island of Guernsey. You don't
remember *Son et Lumière* either? I'm not surprised. It
enjoyed quite a vogue a few years ago, but then I got
involved and, in Britain, we have not seen or heard much of
it since.

I think of *Son et Lumière* as a history lesson in the rain.
The idea – a sound and light show that tells the story of a
building of note – was conceived forty years ago by a
Frenchman, Paul Robert-Houdin, who was caught in a
thunderstorm near a château in the Loire, impressed by the
dramatic effect of the lightning flashing on the building, and
decided to attempt to recreate the effect electronically. His
first production took place at Chambord in 1952. I got
involved some twenty years later when I was introduced to

91

one of his disciples, Joy Masefield, a lovely lady, very English, bird-like and angular, a geography don's wife (I'd have Celia Johnson to play her in the movie), and her own protégé, a bright young electronics engineer, Colin Sanders, wiry, bespectacled, earnest and eager (he'll be played by Rick Moranis). Joy and Colin were staging modest *Son et Lumière* productions of their own at local churches, but had ambitions for Better Things and cottoned on to the idea that all they needed to bring about the Big Break was the involvement of someone with the entrepreneurial zeal and youthful flair for showmanship of yours truly (to be played by Tom Cruise).

We persuaded the city of Leeds to back our first venture. Sir Michael Redgrave and Cyril Fletcher led our cast of distinguished voices. Temple Newsam House, birthplace of Lord Darnley and the original of Templestowe in *Ivanhoe*, provided the venue. While Michèle did the historical research, the script was written by Joy Masefield – whose first name I had printed very small on the posters and whose surname appeared in massive type in the hope that our potential customers might think the poet laureate had had a hand in our endeavours. I am not sure who was responsible for the weather, but whoever it was, was not on our side.

We had anticipated rain, which is why we had erected a solid awning over the auditorium. However, we had not expected *hail*, and when the hail came, and in Leeds that August we felt it came most nights, the clatter of the hailstones on the corrugated iron roof of the auditorium was such that those few who had braved the elements to make the pilgrimage to Temple Newsam for our aptly entitled presentation of *The East Blows Cold* asked for their money back. They could just about see the *Lumière* through the downpour, but the *Son* was drowned out completely.

We moved down south and up market for our next production, an all-star (Peggy Ashcroft, Claire Bloom, John Gielgud, Alec Guinness, as well as Cyril) spectacular at

Royal Greenwich under the auspices of the Department of the Environment who suggested that an outdoor presentation called for sturdy seating beneath a corrugated iron roof. Oh no, we said, it may hail. The DoE were doubtful. We were adamant. We wanted a tarpaulin roof and a tarpaulin roof is what we had. At least, it is what we had until halfway through the second performance when a gigantic gust of wind dislodged the entire roof from its moorings and brought it crashing down on the heads of our unhappy patrons. A few stayed to hear the mellifluous tones of Sir John as 'Time' and to witness the thrilling effect of light playing on the old observatory in the distance, but most came to their senses and went home.

I came to my senses too. The climate was against us. (It's interesting that this thought doesn't appear to have occurred to the team behind Euro-Disney.) I felt Joy Masefield's heart was no longer in it. I reckoned Colin Sanders was a small-time sound engineer on a hiding to nothing. I bid my partners farewell and we all moved on. A few years later I discovered Colin was now worth £50 million.

How did he do it? Since he's a good friend you can poodle down to his villa in the South of France and ask him yourself. Let me hazard three reasons:

He's a worker
The idle rich is an oxymoron, one of those self-contradictory conjunctions like 'military intelligence' or 'humble backbencher' or, these days, 'Royal Family'. Some of those with inherited wealth may be rich and idle, but I have not met a self-made millionaire who wasn't an indefatigable worker. Very few have been to university, but all seem familiar with the Book of Proverbs, Chapter 6, Verses ten and eleven: 'A little sleep, a little slumber, a little folding of the hands to rest and poverty will come upon you like a vagabond and want like an armed man.'

He's ruthlesss
That's not to say he isn't thoughtful, generous and kind – as well as ruthless. The successful are single-minded. They know what they want and they go for it. They take tough decisions, sooner rather than later. Right or wrong, they're resolute. If something (or someone) isn't working, make a change and make it now. (Don't keep your fingers crossed and hope things will get better. They never do.)

He's a genius
Ah, the tricky bit. Mark Twain's definition of genius as ninety-nine per cent perspiration and one per cent inspiration is all very well for Mark Twain. He had the one per cent and a little bit besides. What do you do if you are merely mortal? You could do worse than accept that, in commercial terms, genius and innovation frequently go hand in hand.

Colin was a ruthless workaholic with a genius for creating innovative sound desks that you will now find in recording studios around the world. I am just sorry that when we were partners and in our early twenties I didn't see the potential. It was the same with Richard Branson. We were both teenagers. I was editing the school magazine. He was planning to launch a national magazine for students. We met in a house in Paddington to talk about pooling resources. I sensed he was going somewhere, but it wasn't where I was going and we parted company. It was about the time Michèle came across Andrew Lloyd-Webber. She said, 'I've just met this funny little guy who says he's writing a musical based on a story from the Bible. I ask you!' As I write, a quarter of a century later, *Joseph and His Amazing Technicolour Dreamcoat* is still playing to capacity at the London Palladium.

Yes, the rich are different from us, they have more money, but they are human none the less. They may have unreal lifestyles (and taste that isn't quite yours or mine), but the seriously-rich-of-their-own-making that I have encountered seem rooted in reality: unpretentious, uncomplicated, unphoney. Robert Maxwell was different. Two of his children, Philip and Anne, were contemporaries of ours at Oxford and my first encounter with the bouncing Czech was at a splendid party at his house where, I am ashamed to say, I was attempting to amuse a group of fellow guests with an impersonation of our host when a heavy hand landed on my left shoulder. I spun round to find myself face to face with the great tycoon. I blanched. He looked stern, then he let out a loud, alarming, barking laugh, shook me by the shoulder, turned and walked away. His children were devoted to him, and he must have had real friends, although whenever I was at his house I found the fellow guests spent much of their time talking about him in hushed undertones. At the last party I attended at Headington Hill Hall for what seemed like 2,000 of his closer chums, I noticed he had equipped himself with personal amplification. He was wearing a radio microphone and there were speakers scattered about the house and marquees, so, without having to raise his voice, he could speak discreetly to a single individual or address the multitude at will.

Not long before his death (and, do you remember, we saw the *Lady Ghislaine* when we were on Colin's boat off Cap d'Antibes?) Michèle and I had supper with Anne Maxwell in her flat near Holland Park. Ian and Kevin were there and, at about eleven-thirty, when we were set to go home, they got up and announced that they had to go back to the office.

'But it's nearly midnight,' I protested.

'That means it's nearly five in Mexico and I'm expecting a call,' said Kevin.

'We're tying up a deal,' said Ian with an easy smile.

It seemed like play-acting at the time. Now I expect they wish it had been.

Before becoming a member of parliament I enjoyed the occasional high-earning year, but regardless of my income I have an uncanny knack for spending marginally more than I earn. This seems to be a family characteristic. (Come to think of it, looking at the PSBR, it seems to be a national characteristic.) The last Brandreth to make serious money (and the first, as it happens) was my great-great-great-grandfather, Dr Benjamin Brandreth, who set off to make his fortune in the New World in 1835 and did exactly that. His father and grandfather were also medical men and Benjamin took with him a plentiful supply of the family's well-established patent medicine, Brandreth's Pills, a simple laxative to you and me, but a powerful cure-all when marketed by Dr B. Each packet of pills came with a promise: 'That Brandreth's Pills, in all future time, are warranted to possess and contain those purgative, those cleansing and innocent qualities, which they have always heretofore possessed in so eminent a degree.'

Whatever your problem, pleurisy, inflammation, fever, heart complaint, cancer even, Brandreth's Pills would help not hinder. 'The great advantage of using Brandreth's Pills in sickness is that they *never make any mistakes*, often prolonging, never shortening life.' To prove the point Brandreth published a book packed with hundreds of testimonials from satisfied patients and their awe-struck physicians.

Louisville, November 16, 1837

Sir, I feel it a duty which I owe, not only to you but to the public generally, to acknowledge the great benefit which I have derived from the use of your Pills. I was attacked about six weeks since with chills and fever, from which I recovered in about three weeks, when I was almost immediately attacked with a bilious fever, from which I had great doubts of ever recovering. Fortunately, I was induced by some of my friends to give Brandreth's Pills a trial; and I now find myself perfectly restored in health. After finding the happy effects of these Pills upon myself, I was induced to give them to one of my children – a girl eight years old – who had been ill for some time, apparently in a decline. It gives me pleasure to inform you that she is gradually getting better since we first used the Pills, and I hope in another week to apprise you of her complete recovery.

I am, sir, very respectfully yours,
Felix Wood.

Brandreth had a good product, but he wasn't alone in that. Dr Thomas Beecham's pills were 'Worth a Guinea a Box'; Dr Henry Hembold billed himself as the 'Prince of Druggists'; Dr Joseph Schenck offered a range of efficacious remedies, including Seaweed Tonic, Mandrake Pills and Pulmonic Syrup. Brandreth's Pills were not innovatory: Dr Brandreth's marketing of them was. He was a pioneer of newspaper advertising. He shared the philosophy of his friend and contemporary, PT Barnum: 'Advertising is like learning – a little is a dangerous thing. The reader of a newspaper does not see the first insertion of an ordinary advertisement; the second insertion he sees, but does not read; the third insertion he reads; the fourth insertion he looks at the price; the fifth insertion, he speaks of it to his wife; the sixth insertion he is ready to purchase; and the seventh insertion he purchases.'

The insertions for Brandreth's Pills appeared not once, but thousands of times. Brandreth spent more, far more, than anyone had ever spent on newspaper advertising, and it worked. The fame of his Pills spread far and wide and by the time he died in 1880 the *New York Times* credited him with a personal fortune of a million dollars. He had two wives and fourteen children, one of whom, Henry, was sent back to Cheshire to run the English end of the business. Unhappily, Henry appears to have run it into the ground and to have run through his own share of the family fortune too. By the turn of the century he was negotiating for more funds from New York and being urged by his son, my grandfather (by then a solicitor), to temper his extravagance:

20 Exchange Street, Liverpool
21st January, 1902

My Dear Father,
I have nothing to report with reference to negotiations for loan, but I think that if in the meantime you will consider the following figures you will see that your estimate of £2,400 a year for living expenses is very liberal ...

It was indeed at a time when £50 per annum was for many a working wage. My grandfather was urging his papa to try to make do with no more than nine servants. 'It is just a matter of prudent house-keeping,' as the family's financial adviser is reputed to have counselled Lord Curzon in comparable (if significantly grander) circumstances. The first Marquess Curzon of Kedleston had nine staff in the kitchen alone. 'Does your lordship really require the services of a *second* pastry chef?' 'So it has come to this,' sighed Curzon, 'a fellow's not even to be allowed a biscuit with his sherry. Bah!'

George Nathaniel Curzon was a Tory grandee of the old school. Viceroy of India, Foreign Secretary, and very possibly, had he not been in the House of Lords, Prime Minister instead of Stanley Baldwin in 1923, he had the Grand Manner. His style was evident even as an undergraduate:

> My name is George Nathaniel Curzon,
> I am a most superior person.
> My cheeks are pink, my hair is sleek,
> I dine at Blenheim once a week.

Not for Curzon the classless society. For a number of years he was Chancellor of Oxford University and when, in 1921, Queen Mary was to be entertained at his old college, Balliol, he was asked to approve the proposed menu in advance. He returned it to the Bursar with the single comment: 'Gentlemen do not take soup at luncheon'.

One evening, a little before the outbreak of the Great War, he and a friend were strolling down Regent Street when they came upon the window of Garrards, the jewellers. They paused to take in the range of gold and silverware on display and Curzon's eye was caught by a small silver cylindrical object nestling on a tiny blue cushion at the rear of the window.

'What's that?' he asked his companion.

'What?'

'That, up there,' said Curzon, pointing to the piece of silver.

'Why, Curzon,' said his friend, 'that's a napkin ring.'

'What on earth is a "napkin ring"?' enquired Curzon.

'Surely you've come across a napkin ring before now, Curzon?'

'No, no, truly, I haven't. Pray, what does it do?'

'Well,' said his companion, 'there are some people who cannot afford fresh linen at every meal, so that after breakfast they will take their napkin and fold it not once, but twice, and then roll it into a tube and insert the napkin into that silver ring to keep the same napkin to use again at luncheon.'

Curzon shook his head, sighed and gazed intently at the little silver napkin ring. 'Can there be *such* poverty?'

Lord Curzon inherited his wealth and you can see how it spoilt him. I wouldn't want that to happen to you, my boy. For your own good, your mother and I will be spending while we may to ensure that it doesn't.

NAME-DROPPING

'When people have heard of you, favourably or not, they change.'
John Steinbeck

Noel called. 'I want you both to come and have dinner at the Garrick. I want you to meet Miguel.'

'Is he a waiter?' I asked.

'Don't be stupid,' snapped Noel. 'He's an actor – and he's brilliant. A lot of profile, not a lot of English. How are you on Friday week?'

'The thirteenth? Perfect.'

'Excellent. Seven-thirty. It's the Garrick, so no funny jumpers, thank you.'

When Friday the thirteenth came round Aphra had tonsillitis. This was a dozen or so years ago when she was just a toddler and a responsible parent (ie your mother) knew she shouldn't be left with the baby-sitter. I suggested we call Noel and cancel.

'No,' said Michèle, 'Noel wants you to meet Miguel and you're looking forward to it. You have a night out with the boys.'

I did. I arrived at the Garrick promptly at 7.30 pm and found Noel in the dining room, checking the table arrangements. I broke the news about Michèle. Noel murmured sympathetically and asked the waitress to reset the table. We climbed the stairs to the bar where he had a bottle of the club champagne already on ice.

'No Miguel?' I asked.

'He's parking the car,' said Noel, 'he won't be a minute.'

Forty-five minutes later Miguel had still not appeared and Noel ordered a second bottle of champagne. This one slipped down even more smoothly than the first. (I recall one of my favourite characters in CP Snow insisting that one should always have champagne before dinner. I imagine he meant a glass rather than a bottle.)

A little before nine we finished the second bottle and Noel said brightly, 'Forget Miguel, dinner is served.' And what a splendid dinner it was. At least, I imagine the dinner was splendid. I only remember the wines: a pleasing Petit Chablis to get us started, an outstanding Chambolle-Musigny to keep us going, and a sensational Château Yquem to finish us off. We were just draining our penultimate glasses of the liquid gold when Miguel appeared. He was as I had imagined, in his late twenties, tall, slim, sallow, saturnine. The profile was certainly strong, the English undeniably weak. He did not explain why it had taken him three hours to park the car. Noel didn't ask. Indeed, Noel paid him scant attention, but poured us each a final glass of wine and began to talk to me more animatedly than he had done all evening. He was reaching the tag-line of one of the best of his stories about Coral Browne when Miguel nudged him.

Noel sighed, his eyes narrowed and out of the corner of his mouth he said to me, 'Perhaps he is a waiter after all. There's a school in Milan where they teach waiters how to interrupt stories just as you get to the pay-off.' He turned to Miguel, 'Yes?'

'Noel, isn't that Sir Olivier?' asked Miguel, eyes ablaze with excitement, pointing to the central table at the head of which was sitting the frail figure of Baron Olivier of Brighton, OM.

'Yes, of course,' said Noel wearily. 'This is the Garrick.'

Olivier must have heard his name because he looked up

and looked around. When he saw Noel, Noel offered him a discreet wave and a respectful nod. Olivier brought his fingers slowly to his lips and blew Noel an elaborate yet delicate kiss. Miguel squealed with pleasure.

'A glass of port, I think, don't you?' said Noel, rising lightly from the table and leading me into the hall where we positioned ourselves on a leather sofa, with Miguel standing sentinel at our side. Noel moved on to a story about Godfrey Tearle and Jill Bennett as we sipped our port and watched familiar faces come and go.

At one stage he pottered off to recharge our glasses and, as he returned, Earl Mountbatten of Burma and Sir Richard Attenborough appeared at the top of the stairs and crossed the hallway towards us.

'Ah,' cried Noel, 'the two Dickies together at last!' He pulled me to my feet, 'Gentlemen, may I present my good friend, Mr Gyles Brandreth.' Mountbatten and Attenborough looked appropriately impressed, murmured pleasantries, and moved on.

'Who that with Sir Hattenbrow?' ventured Miguel.

'Royalty,' said Noel, in his best Coward voice.

'I would like to meet a king,' said Miguel a little wistfully.

Noel ignored this, drained his glass, and announced, 'I believe it's time for a nightcap. Follow me!'

As we made our way down the front steps of the Garrick Club, a glossy limousine drove up, the door swung open and out stepped Yul Brynner. Noel yanked my arm and we fell to our knees at Brynner's feet. With a deep salaam Noel cried, 'Welcome to England, O King of Siam.'

I believe we ended up at a nightclub called Heaven where I have a faint recollection of waiters dressed in silk shorts floating about on roller skates. I got home a little before dawn to find Aphra still had tonsillitis and I had the hiccups.

There is a coda to the story. A week or two later Michèle and I happened to be having supper with Lord George Brown and his family, near neighbours of ours in Notting

Hill Gate. On the wagon or off it (and he was on it that night) George liked to reminisce, and his long-suffering wife, Sophie, (who had suffered much and was to suffer more) liked, quite gently, to put him down. He had talked of Ernest Bevin (with respect and affection), he had talked of John Kennedy (with admiration and awe), now he was talking of Harold Wilson (with none of the foregoing). He was lambasting Wilson's presidential style of government, rehearsing the reasons for his resignation as Foreign Secretary, reminding us that he had received more than a thousand letters of support from members of the public. The people had wanted *him* as Prime Minister.

'Now, George,' ventured Sophie.

'It's true,' he asserted, 'and if proof were needed I was at a dinner at the Garrick Club only the other evening when this distinguished-looking fellow, never seen him before, came up to me out of the blue and said, "George, you're the greatest Prime Minister we never had!" '

'Oh, George,' said Sophie, 'he was drunk.'

'No he was not,' protested George.

'He most certainly was. I saw him and his friend on their knees on the pavement not half an hour later, drunk as lords!'

Fortunately, as Sophie had emerged from the Club and witnessed Noel and me staggering to our feet and wandering off towards Heaven, she hadn't caught sight of our faces. My secret was safe – not, frankly, that it would have mattered a jot if she had recognised me on my one and only night of inebriation. Her husband, at his best a formidable political animal who talked a lot of sense, had been drunk most nights of his adult life.

George's drinking foreshortened that life as it had damaged his career. Even in the era of a more circumspect press his alcoholic excesses were common knowledge, thanks mainly, it must be said, to his own indiscretions. On the whole the press treated him kindly. Today he would have stood much less of a chance.

Remember, my boy, if you go into a line of business where fame, or familiarity, or, worst of all, notoriety, are likely to be part of the package, there is a price to be paid. Fame for fame's sake is worthless. It doesn't even get you a better table in the restaurant. It may get you a more conspicuous table, but that's to the restaurateur's benefit not yours.

In schools I sometimes ask students, 'What do you want to be?' expecting them to say 'a lawyer', hoping they'll say 'an engineer'. All too often they say 'rich and famous'. Rich? Yes, there are advantages, freedom from money worries being the principal one. (Who said, 'Money is the sixth sense which enables us to enjoy the other five'?) But, fame? Forget it. I know people – decent people, friends – who are hooked on fame, press-cutting junkies, who phone the gossip columns with stories about themselves as though they need to see their names and faces in print to be reassured that they exist and have worth.

Celebrity for its own sake is worthless. Now and again you may need to court it – to sell your book or your film or your cause – but remember that in the Street of Shame the traffic flows both ways. If you want a good press some days for your own good reasons, bear in mind that the reptiles may give you a bad one some day for theirs. To a journalist, said Fred Allen, 'a human being is an item with skin wrapped around it'. And if you think you can win with the press, think again. When my excursion to Copenhagen with Lord Longford landed me on the front pages and I was plagued with reporters for the first time in my life, the best of them, Nicholas Tomalin, told me, 'If you don't want to say anything just say, "I'll give you a statement if you quote it in full. Here it is: Bugger off!"' ' Trouble is, today they'd print it in full. You can't win and no one is immune. One day even Kenneth Branagh will get a bad press. (Okay, now I've gone too far – but you take my point?)

One lovely thing did happen to me as a result of my time as a minor celebrity, slightly well-known for being slightly well-known. Towards the end of 1982 I received a letter from The Cupola and Tower of the Winds, Belmont Road, Hastings, East Sussex:

Dear Mr Brandreth,
Would you come to Hastings for four hours, or less, to let me paint you as we talk, with something to eat from my wife, Patti, on the side? No commercial considerations at all.
    Let me elaborate and explain.
    I believe the Individual is an endangered species with the advance of the collectivist state and the rapid materialisation of Orwell's 1984; and for years I've been painting Individuals from life – Paul McCartney, the Queen Mother, Sir Alec Guinness. I'd very much like to meet you and paint you.

                                            Yours sincerely,
                                            John Bratby

Bratby didn't drop names, he collected them. Over a period of years he sent the same irresistible letter to hundreds of variegated names culled from *Who's Who* (and, I suspect, *TV Times*) and hundreds of the more vainglorious of us made the pilgrimage to The Cupola and Tower of the Winds where John, looking exactly like Raymond Briggs's Father Christmas in mufti, engaged us in small-talk as, thick and fast, he piled the paint upon the canvas (mostly orange and red and green in my case) and produced a disconcerting image of oneself that one was under no obligation to buy. Forty-eight hours after the sitting a further letter arrived:

Dear Gyles,
It was very amusing to see you and very amusing to paint you and extremely amusing to converse with you. Life is not quite as amusing now that you have departed.

However we will soldier on with fortitude.

I have a duty to offer you the portrait before anyone else and before exhibiting. It is £350. It can be framed and delivered now and one day I would like to borrow it for an exhibition.

Yours,
John

I thought the line about the exhibition a particularly deft touch. I didn't buy the portrait. I didn't like it, nor did Michèle, but I liked John and I liked Patti. Patti was integral to the sitting. Invariably dressed in leather to please the great man (and half-undressed in leather in some of his last, most striking images of her in flagrantly raunchy pose in Venice and Paris and Istanbul), Patti greeted you at the front door and led you up the stairs and along the landing (crowded with canvases of your predecessors) into the studio where John sat you in the chair almost as soon as he had greeted you, quizzed you like an inscrutable old gnome and set to work at once. Patti offered tea or coffee and a bacon sandwich and then retreated to the kitchen where she remained on call – and called she was, quite frequently. Without explanation John would put down his palette knife and call urgently, 'Blue slip! Blue slip!' Patti would come scurrying into the room, glance at the work, and scribble something on a small piece of blue notepaper which she handed to her husband without saying a word. Later in our friendship I asked John about these 'blue slips'. He told me they offered critical advice. The ones I saw contained only encouragement, 'Brilliant', 'This is wonderful', 'I love you'.

It was an extraordinary love-match. They met through the Lonely Hearts column in *Time Out*. She was his muse and his ideal model. Between March and November 1990 he painted eighty different canvases of her, four-foot by three-foot, in assorted pin-up poses, reminiscent, as he said, of Betty

Grable. She had become 'a fantasy being, yet only she would do. No other female. It was essential it was the woman I knew and loved.'

Bratby put obsessive energy into his work. In the late seventies and in the eighties he painted over a thousand individual portraits, some remarkable, none without interest. I have the picture he did of Cyril Fletcher, which Cyril never liked ('makes me look like a spiv'), and I covet his portrait of Kenneth Williams, which at the time (1976) Kenneth adored but couldn't afford: 'It is a marvellous portrait of me! He captured the aspiration, the theatricality, the arrogance and the "boyish" aspect. I was staggered by the cleverness and speed of it!' The prodigious output took its toll. Occasionally a sitter would arrive and John simply didn't have the strength to undertake the work.

Patti sustained the artist and she sustained the sitters. The day I went for my portrait I was on my diet (see page 61) so I had to resist the bacon sandwich. When I came to sign the visitors' book I noticed that in their inscription almost all my predecessors had chosen to concentrate their remarks on the sandwich rather than the portrait, a reflection neither of John's work nor of Patti's cuisine, but of the problem of assessing another's image of oneself. ('O wad some Pow'r the giftie gie us, To see oursels as others see us!')

I saw John as an original, a rare talent and, as I have found is often the case with declared misanthropists, a good companion. Over the last ten years of his life, the Bratbys and the Brandreths shared some memorably convivial outings. John lived to paint, but he also painted to live and when the pictures sold well he lived well. In the spring of 1991 the National Portrait Gallery staged a retrospective of his work and, on the day of the opening, John and Patti entertained us to an over-the-top lunch at the Savoy, so over-the-top that by the time the fellow from *Kaleidoscope* turned up to record the retrospective radio interview for the BBC John was tucked up in his suite sleeping off the effects of his own handsome hospitality. He drained his glass as well as himself and in July 1992, on the day after his sixty-fourth birthday, his heart gave up on him.

I once asked David Frost what he hoped to be remembered for. 'Ever,' he said. Bratby was less ambitious, but I have a hunch that some of his work – the early kitchen sink pictures, some of those sunflowers, one or two of the portraits, the best of the Venice paintings – will outlive the 'fame' of most of his celebrated sitters.

ORATORY

'A speech is a solemn responsibility. The man who makes a bad thirty-minute speech to two hundred people wastes only a half hour of his own time. But he wastes one hundred hours of the audience's time – more than four days – which should be a hanging offence.'

Jenkin Lloyd Jones

George Brown and I worked together on a book to which we gave the sonorous title, *The Voice of History*. It contained what we reckoned were the golden moments from some of the most resonant speeches of all time, from Elizabeth I in August 1588 addressing her troops at Tilbury as the Armada was sailing up the Channel ('I know that I have the body of a weak and feeble woman, but I have the heart and stomach of a King, and of a King of England too ...') to John Kennedy's inaugural address as President of the United States in January 1961 ('And so, my fellow Americans, ask not what your country can do for you; ask what you can do for your country ...'). As the publishers were anxious to maximise our transatlantic sales, there was pinchbeck among the gold (Richard Nixon addressing the men on the moon, Jimmy Carter addressing the men on the ground), and at every turn we were confronted with the problem that a book of speeches – a *written* record of the *spoken* word – is really a contradiction in terms.

Occasionally, but only occasionally, we came across speeches that read as well as they sounded. The most eloquent example is the extraordinary speech delivered to a crowd of some two hundred thousand by Martin Luther King, on 28 August 1963, at a civil rights demonstration in Washington DC ('I have a dream ...'). The passion, the power, the poetry, especially the poetry, work as well on the page as they do if you listen to a recording. It is a beautifully crafted piece of work and builds to an almost miraculous crescendo of emotion and rhetoric:

'Let freedom ring from the snowcapped Rockies of Colorado!
Let freedom ring from the curvaceous peaks of California!
But not only that; let freedom ring from Stone Mountain of Georgia!
Let freedom ring from every hill and mole hill of Mississippi. From every mountainside, let freedom ring.
When we let freedom ring, when we let it ring from every village and every hamlet, from every state and every city, we will be able to speed up that day when all of God's children, black men and white men, Jews and Gentiles, Protestants and Catholics, will be able to join hands and sing in the words of that old Negro spiritual, "Free at last! Free at last! Thank God, almighty, we are free at last!" '

King's oratory will stand the test of time. So will Churchill's. But again and again, George and I found ourselves turning up the transcript of a speech that had long been spoken of with awe as a fabled masterpiece of the orator's art only to find that whatever it was that had brought the audience of an earlier era to their feet now seemed fairly leaden on the printed page. Oddly, the converse proved true too. There are speeches that read well that may not have gone down so brilliantly on the night. The most startling example of this is one of the most celebrated speeches on record, President Abraham Lincoln's address at the dedication ceremony of the National Cemetery at Gettysburg in November 1863: 'Fourscore and seven years ago our fathers brought forth upon this continent a new nation ...'. The words of the Gettysburg Address have echoed down the years, but apparently the correspondent of *The Times* caught the mood of the occasion in his report: 'The ceremony was rendered ludicrous by some of the sallies of that poor President Lincoln.... Anything more dull and commonplace it wouldn't be easy to imagine.' 'Who cares what *The Times* says?' says you, and quite right too. However damning the press, however fawning and flattering the hangers-on, in his gut the speaker knows how his speech went. This was Lincoln's immediate verdict: 'That speech fell on the audience like a wet blanket. I am distressed about it. I ought to have prepared it with more care.'

The senior politician today has the task of making his or her speeches serve several purposes simultaneously. One and the same speech has to work in different ways, delivering the goods for the record, for those in the hall, for those watching and listening on television or radio, for the editor choosing the sound-bite. (One of the incidental pleasures of helping draft Party Conference speeches is crafting the potential sound-bites and then seeing how many get used. My experience suggests that news editors are as predictable as politicians' clichés.) Constructing, writing and delivering a speech that fulfils all the requirements is no easy task, and, while there are rules that will help reduce the risk of failure, there are none that guarantee success. A successful speech is not about the specifics of content or form, but about impact. That is why speakers of markedly contrasting styles can be equally effective.

Of the celebrated orators he had heard over many years George Brown ranked Churchill and Aneurin Bevan as the most formidable. Harold Macmillan he dismissed as a complete phoney, 'all histrionics and ham acting', but with Churchill's carefully studied, painstakingly rehearsed orations, there was matter as well as manner. Of Nye Bevan's speeches outside the Commons there is little record because when he spoke from the platform he spoke spontaneously, not without a structure to his speech but without notes. Bevan's facility had its own dangers. George told me that Nye's pleasure in phrase-making on the flood ('always a great part of his charm even when I most disagreed with what he was saying') led him into rhetorical excesses which provoked unjustified misunderstanding, mistrust, 'even hatred'. The famous example was when Bevan was held to have described the middle classes as 'lower than vermin', an allusion he denied – he was referring solely to the Tory Party! – but from which, according to George, he never escaped since the speech was unscripted and unrecorded and there was little he could do to set the record straight.

George maintained that the single most brilliant speaker he had heard was Professor Harold Laski, one of the leading socialist thinkers in the thirties and forties, who broke all the rules of public speaking, and delivered every speech as a lecture, with the minimum of movement, one hand fixed on his lapel, the other locked in his jacket pocket throughout, the voice grating, almost monotonous, but the logic, wit and presentation overwhelmingly compelling.

From George's description I would judge that Laski's oratory was of a similar temper to that of Enoch Powell. Around the House of Commons, in all the offices and corridors, in the library, the restaurants and tea room, there are television screens that show the name of the member who at that moment is addressing the House. (They also indicate the present time and the time when the member began to speak.) When I arrived I asked longer-serving members what names appearing on the screen would induce them to put down their papers or their tea cups and wander into the Chamber. Powell was the name most frequently mentioned. Today, if you polled the current members and asked them which of their number would be most likely to bring them in, I imagine Tony Benn would come top of the list. Benn's own verdict is that it is 'sincerity rather than oratory that defines a

Above 1950: GB and friend at Hanover Zoo

Below 1969: 'I know how to show a girl a good time.' GB and Michèle
enjoy the Swinging Sixties

Above 1968: GB selects Lady Annunziata Asquith as Oxford's 'Miss Zuleika Dobson'

Below 1968: Diana Quick, Sir Michael Redgrave, Archie Harradine (who wrote the script) and GB on the first night of *Cinderella*

Left 1968: GB addresses the Oxford Union, with William Waldegrave (now Chancellor of the Duchy of Lancaster) and Edwina Cohen (now Mrs Currie) looking on

Below 1970: 'So you dropped Yehudi Menuhin's Stradivarius, eh?!' The Archbishop of Canterbury enjoys the joke

Above 1973: GB, in disguise, in a Birmingham bookshop, warming up the punters for Eric Thompson (Emma's dad)

Below 1973: 'A tarpaulin roof for the auditorium – what a good idea!' GB, Dame Peggy Ashcroft, Cyril Fletcher and Michèle at a *Son et Lumière* script conference

Above 1974: Tony Britton and Celia Johnson in *The Dame of Sark* at the Oxford Theatre Festival

Right 1983: 'Weren't you the worst Malvolio I ever saw?' Sir Michael Hordern recognises GB while Ronnie Barker contemplates retirement at the Oxford Playhouse Diamond Jubilee

Above 1977: Wholesome family
entertainment with plenty of sparkle
– GB and Bonnie Langford in the
Puzzle Party Christmas Special

Left 1987: A notion at ease with
itself: one man and his jumpers

Above 1985: Spot the rat! The TV-am team celebrates its second birthday

Below 1986: The *Countdown* final. 'I know it's only a game, but at least one of us went to the right university.' (Carol Vordermann and Richard Whiteley went to Cambridge.)

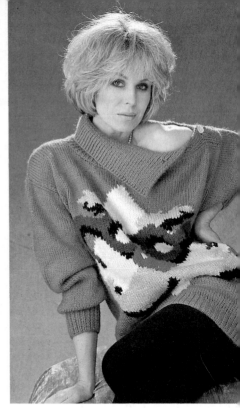

Above Two friends in jumpers: Jane Asher and Joanna Lumley

Below Two friends with cigars: Simon Cadell and (masquerading as Edward VII) Noel Davis

Above 1976: GB's first attempt
n the record for the longest after-
inner speech (Gayle Hunnicutt in
attendance)

Above 1982: GB's final attempt
(NPFA's director Bob Satterthwaite
and Kenneth Williams in attendance)

Below 1983: Unveiling Andrew Festing's painting at Buckingham Palace
(Prince Philip in attendance)

Above 1984: Ringo Starr, Haro[ld] Wilson and GB looking round f[or] someone *really* famous to talk to

Left 1990: 'The 2.30 at Sandow[n] Park looks promising, Ma'am.' HM The Queen and GB in search [of] small-talk

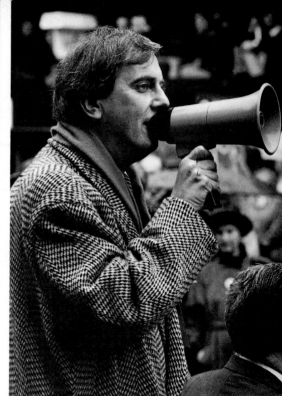

Above 1964: 'Vote for Sir Alec!'   *Above* 1992: 'Vote for John Major!'

Below 1992: 'Vote for Gyles Brandreth!' The Prime Minister comes to
Chester

Best friends: GB and Michèle at the Teddy Bear Museum, Stratford-upon-Avon

great speech – when what someone's saying is rooted in his life and convictions – sincerity, and in a funny way modesty.'

I am a novice in the House of Commons (and as nervous as the rest of them; one of the early surprises was to see how the hands of many of the most seasoned Commons performers shake throughout their speeches), but in other, less alarming, arenas I have been banging on for years. I turned professional at nineteen. By a series of happy chances during that nine months in America between school and university I found myself addressing, first, for $50, a conference of teachers at the New York Hilton and, next, for $60, one thousand girls and fifty nuns at a convent in Baltimore. Since that baptism of fire in the sixties I have given thousands of speeches in hundreds of settings in a variety of countries. (The worst experience was at a lush hotel in Switzerland where I was addressing a conference of fertiliser salesmen and throughout my speech had the deeply unhappy and profoundly sozzled wife of the Chairman on my left tugging relentlessly at my dinner jacket and bleating, 'Why aren't you looking at me now? I was good enough over dinner! Why won't you talk to me now? Look at me, look at me, look – at – me!' Sitting the other side of this tragic but, so far as I was concerned, traumatising figure, was the company's Sales Director who clearly felt that gagging the Chairman's wife had not featured in his job description. Eventually, when her shrill lament was actually drowning out my somewhat forced oration (and I had the benefit of a microphone) her husband, who was three seats away, put down his cigar and escorted her briskly out of the room. 'You don't care about me, do you, damn you, Gyles' were the last words she shrieked across the dining room as, lamely, I struggled towards my peroration.) As a rule, seeing members of the audience leaving the room isn't too disconcerting. It's when they start walking towards you that you need to watch out.

At the speaking game not only am I an old hand (or should it be a weary throat?), I even have the doubtful distinction of having held the world record for delivering the longest-ever after-dinner speech, not once, but three times. In 1976 I was approached by Action Research for the Crippled Child, an important and imaginative charity which had come up with the ingenious idea of inviting people to break world records and be sponsored on the charity's behalf in their attempts. The record for the longest after-dinner speech was then held by the Reverend Henry Whitehead who, on 16 January 1874, rose to his feet at the Rainbow Tavern, Fleet Street, and spoke non-stop for three hours. One hundred and two years later I captured the Reverend Whitehead's title by talking for four hours and nineteen minutes at a dinner at the Mayfair Hotel in London. Among the guests was a friend of mine, the host of *Just a Minute*, Nicholas Parsons. I assumed he had simply come to cheer. In fact, he had come to assess the competition, and a year later I found he had wrested the record from me, without deviation, hesitation or repetition. In 1978 Action Research persuaded the pair of us to do it all over again and speak for as long as we could on the same night at the same hotel in adjacent rooms. We each spoke for eleven hours, but the challenge was not thinking what to say, it was getting through the night without going to the loo.

The charity had anticipated our dilemma and, following consultations with John, Bell & Croydon, chemists of Wigmore Street, had thoughtfully equipped us both with (how can I put this delicately?) 'a personal appliance', an elastic belt with, hanging from it, a long rubber tube. Worn beneath the trousers, it was designed as the ultimate portaloo, a personal convenience you can actually wear. As the fitter from John, Bell & Croydon explained with pride, 'It's perfect for taking the salute on cold parade grounds; it really does mean you can perform anywhere.'

When it comes to clothes, my boy, you know the rule: on key occasions never wear something you've not worn before. Don't sport a brand-new suit to a critical interview: wear a good one, but one you know. Unhappily, neither Nicholas nor I heeded this golden rule. We went in to dinner all strapped up and ready for action, secure (and comforted) in the knowledge that if nature called we could answer the call without interrupting our flow (if you see what I mean). Alas, we made one fatal mistake: we had no dry run. (This isn't an easy story to tell, is it?)

Dinner was early so that at 8.00 pm on the dot we could get to our feet in our adjoining rooms and start our marathon rabbit. By midnight we were both in full swing and, because long-distance speaking is thirsty work and we were each equipped with the ultimate security blanket, we were blithely taking regular and hefty sips of water. By 2 am, we had both been spouting for six hours and I was beginning to feel nature calling. Once I had decided the time had come for action, I discovered that relieving yourself in front of a hundred dinner-jacketed charity supporters, even if they don't know you are doing it, doesn't come that naturally, at least not to me. To help me on my way I emptied the carafe, drained the glass, concentrated the mind and glanced to the ground. There, trailing from my trouser leg was a long, a very long, rubber tube. Plunging my hands into my pockets I groped hopefully, but it was too late. The appliance had slipped its mooring and was gently descending my inside leg and making its snakelike way out into the open.

How I survived the next five hours without inflicting permanent personal injury I will never know, but I managed. And so did Nicholas. It turned out that he had lost his appliance within minutes of me losing mine, and at the end of our eleven-hour ordeal we both made our way into *The Guinness Book of Records* and the ground-floor Gents at the Hyde Park Hotel at exactly the same moment. Not since Mafeking has there been a relief like it.

Nicholas and I shared the record for a few years until I made my final assault on it on the night of 3 April 1982 at a dinner in aid of the National Playing Fields Association, generously sponsored by Cockburn's Port who, in return for the £1,000 they were giving to the cause, wanted me to be seen to be sipping their admirable product as the night wore on. Moments before I was due to speak Cockburns proudly presented me with an exceptional port from a vintage year. I thanked them profusely and slipped discreetly to the lavatory where I decanted the vintage wine down the loo (yes, an entire bottle of the 48!) and replaced it with lightly diluted Ribena. I rose to speak at 9.00 pm just as dinner was being cleared away, and sat down again twelve and a half hours later, just as breakfast was being served. What amazed my audience was not that I could talk non-stop for twelve and a half hours, but that I could do so while drinking an entire bottle of port without falling over.

What amazed me about my audience is that they all stayed the course and, more remarkable still, all stayed awake. 'I do not object to people looking at their watches when I am speaking,' said Lord Birkett. 'I strongly object when they start shaking them to make sure they are still going.'

Birkett, a distinguished advocate and a wonderful after-dinner speaker by all accounts, recognised that a successful speech requires a confluence of circumstances: 'the effect achieved depends on the character and quality of the speaker himself, the occasion on which he speaks, the subject matter of the speech and the form in which the speech is cast.' There is no single secret, no one trick of the trade, that will produce the apparently effortless yet totally masterful effect we all yearn for. There are books galore on the art of public speaking (I have written a couple myself) but the best of them don't say much more than the obvious: stand up, speak up, shut up.

I don't know whether public speaking will prove to be part and parcel of your life as it has been of mine, but just in case I offer four quick reminders:

Be aware
Be aware of what you want to achieve. Do you want to leave your audience cheered, cheered up, moved, impressed,

better informed? What is the message you want to convey? What is the impact you want to make? Remember that what you want to hear yourself say may not be what your audience wants to hear. Be aware what you want, but be as keenly aware of what they want too. Once you have decided on the goal of your speech, make sure nothing within it deflects from that end. (During presidential contests in the United States each phrase in each set-piece speech by the main contenders has the 'buzz test' applied to it. Does that passage produce the right kind of buzz in at least one key element of our target audience? If it doesn't, it's a waste of words.)

Be brief
No one ever complained because a speech was too brief. (That's the rule, but there are exceptions. A few years ago, when I was active on the professional speaking circuit, I was booked to perform at a civic dinner in the North East. I remember it because there were large tea cups as well as wine glasses by every place (said the Mayor, 'The wine be for the toasts, the tea be to enjoy') and I gave a thirty-minute address that – though I say it as shouldn't – went tolerably well. As I sat down and the audience rose to cheer, the Mayor's truculent secretary came up behind me and whispered in my ear, 'We booked you for forty minutes. This really won't do.' And she meant it.) It is always best to leave them wanting more and always better to cut much-loved paragraphs in their entirety than gabble through it all at break-neck speed. When speaking take your time, particularly at the beginning. When you stand, pause, take in the room, wait for the hush (yes, wait-for-as-long-as-it-takes) before you start.

Be prepared
I recall having lunch with Sir John Clements when he was appearing in a CP Snow adaptation at the Theatre Royal, Haymarket. It was a matinée day towards the end of the run, but he wouldn't have even a single glass of wine. 'I know the

house will be three-quarters empty,' he said, 'but there may be one person, one lone individual at the back of the dress circle, who has paid good money for her seat and has never seen my work before. She may never see it again, so I want her to have my very best this afternoon.'

For me, total audience awareness requires a totally clear head. Not drinking before speaking is the one rule that in more than a quarter of a century of what feels like non-stop spouting, I have never broken. George Brown told me it wasn't the drink that gave him his most embarrassing moment: it was the fruit. At a lunch in New York for United Nations' ambassadors, as he got to his feet to address the distinguished gathering he plucked a grape from the elegant arrangement on the table in front of him. The toast master had announced him, the room was silent and expectant, and Britain's Foreign Secretary was struggling to extricate his dentures from a piece of fruit made of wax.

Unless you are accustomed to scripting speeches a written text will sound like an essay, which is why I recommend notes rather than a full script. Write them on cards and number the cards, just in case they fall to the floor the moment before you are due on your feet. And if you are offered a microphone use it, or at least appear to use it. People will think they can hear you better if you are standing in front of it. And if it's on while you're speaking make sure it's off before you sit back after your oration and mutter to your neighbour that the audience were a bunch of fools but it seemed to go okay none the less.

Be bold

Dare to be yourself. Don't tell jokes if that's not your style. Don't be formal if you are not inclined. Go as far as you want to go in whatever direction, making sure you are taking the audience with you as you go.

If you summon him, our old friend energy will get you through. I remember sharing a platform with Cecil

Parkinson about ten years ago; it was in the Great Room at
Grosvenor House, with an audience of over a thousand.
Throughout dinner Cecil kept being called away. First he had
to phone the Prime Minister, then he had to call his wife,
next his secretary was on the line, then it was the Prime
Minister once more and then his wife. He must have taken a
dozen calls between the soup and the coffee, but when he got
to his feet his concentration was absolute, his delivery just
right: easy, confident, relaxed. The audience sensed that here
was a man who knew what he was doing and did it with
style. I returned home to Michèle full of enthusiasm,
'Parkinson is extraordinary. He was harried all evening by
call after call and then gave a wonderfully polished turn
before rushing off to Number Ten. Remarkable!' When we
woke up in the morning, we discovered how remarkable:
that was the day the story broke about his affair with Sara
Keays. I salute his professionalism – and his style. In my
constituency earlier this year he gave a delightful speech in
the course of which he recounted the familiar tale of the door-
to-door brush salesman with the roving eye who came home
one evening having mislaid his bicycle. Next morning he
woke with a seraphic smile on his face. When his wife asked
peevishly why he was grinning from ear to ear, the salesman
said, 'I've just remembered where I left my bike!' The
audience in Chester laughed a little nervously. I suspect Cecil
told the story deliberately, just to be wicked. He knows what
they're all thinking.

When I made my final assault on the record for the longest
after-dinner speech Andrew Festing was on hand to
immortalise the occasion in oils. When Michèle and I
attended the Guildhall luncheon marking the fortieth
anniversary of the Queen's accession to the throne, we were
delighted to find Andrew again in attendance – with a slightly
larger canvas this time. This was the day the Queen spoke of
her 'annus horribilis'. Some of the press reports gave the
impression the speech had been a whinge. That wasn't how it

came over to those who were there. To us it seemed open and honest, surprisingly personal, humourous and wry. Her Majesty also set a precedent with the speech. Because she had a filthy cold and a scratchy voice she did what every speaker would like to do and spoke before lunch, not after. She was bold and she was different. It worked. It usually does.

Ps & Qs

'When royalty leaves the room it is like getting a seed out of your tooth.'

Joyce Grenfell's mother, Mrs Paul Phipps

I like the Queen. I like the idea of the Queen. I also like this particular Queen as a person, not, frankly, that you could call our relationship *profound*. Very sweetly she has asked me to a number of her garden parties, but there's always such a crowd, and, candidly, when we have enjoyed a few moments alone together, we have been somewhat lost for words.

I suspect we were both quite tired on the evening we found ourselves stuck together in a corner at a private drinks party. I had had a long day, she has had a long reign, and the consequent conversation was far from free-flowing, more Pinter than Stoppard.

GB: Had a busy day, Ma'am?
HM: Yes. Very.
GB: At the Palace?
HM: Yes.
GB: A lot of visitors?
HM: Yes.
(PAUSE)
GB: The Prime Minister?

HM: Yes.
(PAUSE)
GB: He's very nice.
HM: Yes. Very.
(PAUSE)
GB: I've been to Wimbledon today.
HM (Brightening): Oh, yes?
GB (Brightening too): Yes.
HM:(We're both trying hard now): I've been to
        Wimbledon too.
GB (Exhilarated): Today?
HM: No.
GB: (Well, we tried): No, of course not. (PAUSE) I wasn't at
        the tennis.
HM: No?
GB: No. I was at the theatre. (LONG PAUSE) Have you
        been to the theatre in Wimbledon?
(PAUSE)
HM: I imagine so.
(INTERMINABLE PAUSE)
GB: You know, ma'am, my wife's a vegetarian.
HM: That must be very dull.
GB: And my daughter's a vegetarian too.
HM: Oh dear.

The problem with being the Queen is that people
remember what you say to them. The difficulty in being the
Queen at a private function is that because you are still the
Queen there is an invisible moat around you, so people don't
float up and helpfully move the conversation along, and as
it's a private do there isn't an equerry ever-ready in your
eye-line to come to the rescue as you send out alarm signals
by moving your handbag from one arm to the other.

There is no doubt that night I let my monarch down. And
there is equally no doubt that in over four decades of public
service she has never let her subjects down, not once. It is a

remarkable record: forty years plus and not a foot wrong. (There are some politicians who couldn't get through forty minutes without putting their foot in it.) As an institution the constitutional monarchy continues to serve us well. There are many advantages – political, ceremonial, commercial – to having a non-elected hereditary head of state, as a figurehead, as a tourist attraction, even as a focal point for national gossip. (And on that score, what a lot of sanctimonious tosh has been talked these last few years! Only today I had a letter from a lady click-clicking and tut-tutting about the suitability of the Prince of Wales as a potential head of the established church. As I recall, the Church of England was founded for the personal convenience of Henry VIII who – correct me if I'm wrong – managed to break each of the Ten Commandments several times over during the course of his reign. Despite this inauspicious start both the Church and the monarchy have survived for several hundred years and done the state some service.)

Of course, the Royal Family, or at least some of those in their households, have been guilty of occasional bouts of priggish sanctimoniousness as well. Ten or so years ago I organised a charity night at the theatre and the delightful Princess Alexandra (really normal, really nice) graced us with her presence. Checking out the guest list of those to be presented during the interval drinks, her secretary vetoed one of the suggestions. 'Why?' I asked. 'She's divorced. We prefer to avoid formal presentations to divorcees.' Well, the whirligig of time has since brought in some changes. This year for the garden parties, if you couldn't lay on a spouse, you could bring 'a partner'. Realism is breaking loose in the House of Windsor. The Marquesa de Varela, the caramel-coated toast of *Hello!* magazine, went recently to interview the Princess Royal at Buckingham Place and told the Princess, 'I've come here to do a nice, positive, happy story ...' 'Well,' said Her Royal Highness, 'you've come to the wrong place.'

I have been closer physically to Princess Anne than to any of the other royals. Michèle and I organised a charity dinner at which she was the guest of honour and, as you will discover, my boy, on these occasions attention to detail is important. I attended personally to the detail of the place settings at the top table. The management of the Grosvenor House were not specially amused to see me repolishing their silver, realigning their crystal, readjusting the precise positioning of their chairs, but they put up with it. I have to say that when I had finished the table looked a treat. At the appropriate moment, I ushered HRH to her place, Harold Wilson intoned Grace (it was that sort of occasion), and the flunkies helped us into our seats. As she sat down Princess Anne let out a sharp cry of pain as she cracked her knees against the metal table leg which was positioned *precisely* in front of her chair. Wearing a long dress she was obliged to keep her knees together and had no choice but to tuck them to the right of the table leg where they nestled snugly against mine. Throughout dinner from hip to knee we were as one, which again put something of a dampener on the small-talk.

I am a particular fan of Prince Philip, who has the Geoffrey Johnson-Smith gift of looking forty-five at seventy-two, and who, for nearly half a century, has fulfilled a fairly thankless task with considerable distinction. Just as Harold Wilson's most significant legacy is the Open University, so Prince Philip's will be the Duke of Edinburgh Award Scheme. To have established either is enough of an achievement for one lifetime. (And to be a graduate of either is no mean achievement too. When a pair of candidates of comparable calibre, with similar academic qualifications, walk in for a job interview, if one of them has the Duke of Edinburgh Award on his or her c.v. that candidate gets the job.) Encouraged by Lord Mountbatten, the first national charity that Prince Philip took on after his marriage to Princess Elizabeth in 1947 was the Playing Fields Association, founded in the 1920s as the national trust of recreational space with the aim of ensuring that children of all ages and backgrounds had somewhere safe to play, for sport, for recreation, for letting off steam. During the years in which I have been involved in the charity, latterly as chairman, what impressed me most about Prince Philip as president was not simply his sustained interest in the detail of the subject but that he maintained his curiosity. Forty-six years on, he still wants to know more.

He has also mastered the small-talk. When I became a member of parliament and launched myself on a life that includes its fair share of inconsequential conversation with comparative strangers, he introduced me to an admirable five-word opening gambit that works for all ages and all types on all occasions: 'And what keeps you busy?' (Perhaps I should have tried it on Her Majesty?) Harold Macmillan had a comparable fail-safe phrase, to be trotted out when encountering constituents where the face is vaguely familiar but the detail is missing: 'How's the old trouble then?' (My boy, the time when you definitely need a stock phrase to help you out is when you go to see a friend in the theatre and the show is dire and their performance, if anything, worse. They know you are out front, so when the curtain comes down there's no escape. Given the quality of the evening, 'Darling you were wonderful' is simply not on. Selina Cadell's solution is to walk boldly into the dressing room, wagging a forefinger and declaring, 'Well how about you then?!' David Frost passed on to me Diahann Carroll's version of the same trick. You knock on the door and when the voice within calls 'Come!' you thrust it open, march in with arms outstretched and cry, 'Boy, were you on that stage!')

I have not found going to the theatre with royalty a completely comfortable experience. The royals are inclined to talk through the performance. I think it is well-intentioned – they want you to know they are having a right royal good time – but it is difficult to know how to respond. If you chatter back it encourages them. If you don't it seems discourteous. Sir John Gielgud tells how King George V enjoyed his playgoing 'at the back of the box chatting about racing with Sir Edward Elgar'. The King and Queen Mary went to a matinée of *Hamlet* at the Theatre Royal, Haymarket, and, on arrival, the Queen enquired what time the performance was due to end. 'You see,' she explained, 'the King always has to have his tea punctually, and he is so anxious not to miss the girl with the straws in her hair.'

Sir John's favourite Queen Mary story starts with King George out walking in the garden of Buckingham Palace and asking why his customary equerry was not in attendance. He was told the man was unwell. 'What's wrong with him?' asked the King. 'Oh the universal complaint, sir,' was the guarded reply. Next day Queen Mary remarked to someone, 'I hear His Majesty's equerry is ill. What is the matter with him?' 'A bad attack of haemorrhoids, I'm afraid, ma'am.' 'Oh!' said the Queen, 'why did the King tell me it was the clap?'

If you ask Noel for his favourite Queen Mary story he will probably recall the occasion, towards the beginning of the Second World War, when she was visiting an evacuation station to bring some comfort to a few of the children who had been bombed out of their homes and forced to take refuge there. Having asked a nine-year-old urchin what kept him busy, she enquired of the boy, 'And where do you live?' 'Back 'a Selfridges,' said the lad, 'wha' about you?' Queen Mary was then living at Marlborough House and replied, 'Back 'a Fortnums.'

My favourite royal story is four hundred years old. It is the one John Aubrey tells in *Brief Lives* concerning Edward de Vere, the assiduous courtier of Elizabeth I who was so deeply distressed when he broke wind in the royal presence while executing a low and obsequious bow that he immediately put himself into voluntary exile. When, in due course, after the passage of seven long years, he re-presented himself at court, he was graciously received by the Queen. As he bowed low in obeisance to his sovereign, she said, 'Welcome back, Lord de Vere, we have quite forgot the fart.'

A month or so ago, at an elegant reception in the recently (and beautifully) restored Durbar Room at the Foreign Office, I found myself with a pair of retired but still oh-so-spry diplomats. 'In a long career,' mused the first, 'you are bound to meet any number of remarkable people; some you recall quite vividly, others have slipped your memory completely, but, as a rule, I have found that no one ever forgets their first head of state. Mine was George the Fifth. Who was yours?' he said, turning to his colleague.

'The Emperor Haile Selassie, oddly enough.'

Both of them turned their beady eyes on me. 'And how about you?'

'The President of Switzerland,' I said.

'Ah,' they smiled in unison. 'Yes, of course.'

To have offered Charles de Gaulle would have been quite wrong since, as you'll recall, he cut me, but, for a few hours back in 1965, the President of Switzerland and I were really quite close.

I was seventeen and managed to secure myself a well-paid summer holiday job by default. Actually, it was a case of deflowering rather than default. At school a young master had committed the cardinal sin and developed a *tendresse* for a girl in my class. It was a *tendresse* that turned into a rather hasty wedding during the summer holidays, which meant that the errant teacher was unexpectedly unable to take up his August assignment as tutor to two children in Switzerland. As I was available and willing (he liked his pupils to be available and willing), he passed on the job, and his railway tickets, to me.

I set off from Victoria Station and, eighteen hours later, emerged, bewildered and dishevelled, on the empty platform of Sion Station in the Valais region of Switzerland. I was expecting to be met, but I was not expecting to be met by two smartly uniformed soldiers and a military limousine sporting a fluttering Swiss flag on the bonnet. I sensed immediately that I was underdressed and unprepared for the role I was to undertake. The soldiers sensed it too, but they had their orders and they obeyed them. They saluted me, relieved me of my rucksack, ensconced me in the car and drove me off to my new employer. It turned out that I was to be tutor and companion to the offspring of the head of the Swiss Army, a splendidly grizzled old soldier with a delightfully vivacious second wife. The Brigadier (I believe he was actually a Marshal, but we called him Brigadier) had seen service (if not necessarily very active service) over four decades and was evidently as tough as they come. Our day began at five when he led the entire family out into the woods to gather mushrooms for breakfast. He explained that you had to eat what you picked. He had found this rule very effective in ensuring that his troops learnt quickly and correctly which fungi were poisonous and which were not.

During that August and September we spent time in Berne, time on the road (visiting military establishments, in what seemed like complete villages built within mountains), and time at the Brigadier's holiday retreat in the hills outside Sion. It was to the holiday home that the President of Switzerland came to dinner. He was an old crony of the Brigadier's and it was made clear to 'Madame' (he called his young bride 'Madame') that all that was wanted was something very informal – '*un repas bien simple et puis un jeu de cartes.*' Madame set about preparing the most elaborate simple supper you can imagine. The Brigadier set about teaching me the President's (and his) favourite game of cards.

Even in Switzerland, even when he's an old mucker of your husband's, having the head of state to dinner is none the less an ordeal. There were to be six of us: the President and Madame la Présidente, the Brigadier and Madame, another old soldier (who knew the family and the card game equally well) and me. I am afraid the evening when it came was not a total success, although it taught me several valuable lessons. The culinary calamities included a soufflé that wouldn't rise and savoury jellies that wouldn't set. (Lesson No. 1: When entertaining old soldiers 'safe and simple' is always the better bet. Besides, a simple failure is less noticeable than an elaborate one.) Happily, the wine flowed. (Lesson No. 2: Old soldiers never die, but they are happy to float away.) Unhappily, when one of the bottles was emptied I invited the President's wife to kiss the bottom of it, telling her I had heard that if you did there was an old Swiss tradition that said you would be married within the year. I was meaning to help, but far from lightening the mood this vulgar touch on my part only served to increase the *froideur*. (Lesson No. 3: It is not the duty of the most junior guest to be the life and soul of the party.)

When dinner was over and we men settled down to cards I happened to win the first game – and the second – and, *mon dieu*, the third. (Lesson No. 4: Never play to lose, but don't always play to win. There is a difference.) We had just embarked on a fourth game, and this was the one it looked as if the President might win, when Madame took us by surprise, tinkled a little bell, and suddenly announced the *Son et Lumière*.

'*Quoi?*' barked the Brigadier. '*Le Son et Lumière? Où? Quand?*'

'*Ici! Maintenant!*' simpered Madame.

'*Mais non!*' expostulated the Brigadier.

'*Mais oui!*' cooed Madame.

It transpired that our thoughtful hostess had arranged a command performance of the Sion *Son et Lumière* at 10 pm as a special presidential treat. (Lesson No. 5: Old soldiers don't like surprises. Not many people do. And the more elaborate and carefully prepared the surprise the less welcome it will be.) The Brigadier was not accustomed to his wife taking executive decisions (he told me that when women were first allowed a referendum on whether or not they wanted the vote he had locked Madame in the bathroom for the day), but the President showed the courtesy that becomes a head of state, laid down his cards and got to his feet. (Lesson No. 6: 'Uneasy lies the head that wears the crown.' There is always a price to be paid for life at the top.)

We clambered to the foot of the hill and the President glad-handed the few villagers who had turned out to cheer. The six of us sat together on the same bench to watch the show. It only lasted three-quarters of an hour and it hardly mattered that there was no roof (either tarpaulin or corrugated iron) as the drizzle was light and there were umbrellas for all.

At the end of the performance, the President and his lady applauded gamely, but, despite being pressed, declined the offer of a nightcap and one last game of cards. Somewhat stiffly we all embraced one another and the presidential pair stepped into their motor and were sped away.

By ten the following morning the President's chauffeur was back. Madame answered the front door to find him standing there holding the biggest, most elaborate, grandest, grossest box of chocolates you have ever seen. The moment she set eyes on them, poor Madame burst into tears. (Lesson No. 7: If you overdo the thank-you present you give the game away.)

RULES

'I pray thee cease thy counsel
Which falls into mine ears as profitless
As water in a sieve.'
William Shakespeare, *Much Ado About Nothing*

It wasn't at Rules, but at Simpson's-in-the-Strand nearby, that I learnt not to jump to conclusions. I was sixteen and being entertained to dinner by a beautiful woman old enough to be my mother. As it happens, she was my friend's mother and she was generously giving the pair of us this slap-up nosh as a celebratory post- O-Level treat.

You didn't go to Simpson's for a culinary adventure. You went for potted shrimps, saddle of mutton or pink, tender beef, sliced slantingly down to the bone, with real horseradish sauce, heavy Yorkshire pudding, crisp roasted potatoes, piping hot cabbage, then an Edwardian dessert, followed by a savoury or mature Stilton cheese. You wouldn't find the fripperies of an Escoffier or the super-subtleties of a Raymond Blanc here; nothing foreign or fancy (apart from the wines), even the head chef was called the Master-cook and boasted a dependably English name, Arthur Moss. If you go today you will find a portrait of him in the foyer. When we went in 1964 he was nearing the end of his reign, which had begun in 1940, but, *pace* the Beatles in the hit parade and Betty Friedan in the bestseller lists, at 100 The Strand Mr Moss ensured that the old values were maintained. There was even a dining room downstairs reserved for men only where a gentleman could pretend he was at a London club and sit at the communal table.

We were upstairs, thoroughly enjoying the Great British Tradition, knowing it was an anachronism, relishing it all the same. It was a happy evening, an evening when a sixteen year old could feel secure and sophisticated at the same time. Our glasses were refilled (a deep, warm, comforting claret), we raised them to one another and one of us said – I think it was Henry, it might have been me – 'Here's to the future!' The toast made us all laugh, an easy, comfortable, uncomplicated laugh. I looked at Henry and said, 'We'll toast the present next.' I looked at his mother and thought, 'I know she's thirty-six but she is still extraordinarily beautiful.' And then I felt her hand on my knee.

And all at once my heart stood still. I had no idea – no idea at all – what to do. I looked away. I watched the waiter carving the roast. I couldn't think what to say. I felt I could hear my heart thumping, louder and still louder. I swallowed hard and looked back at her. She smiled and turned to Henry. As she turned her hand travelled up my leg. It stopped. Then it travelled further. I had no choice. Mine went down to meet hers. Without hesitating she took my hand in hers and, to my bewilderment, pressed a florin, an old two shilling coin, into my palm. She turned to look at me and narrowed her eyes gently and slowly in the most soul-melting smile.

My head swam, my mind raced. 'What is going on? Why is she trying to pay me? This is madness!'

Then she took her hand away, leant towards me and whispered in my ear, 'You're supposed to tip the carver.'

Why hadn't my father told me that when you go to Simpson's-in-the-Strand for dinner the senior gentleman present always tips the carver? A son needs a father for advice like that.

My father taught me many things – how to tie a proper

bow tie without looking in the mirror was one of the most useful – but he was no Lord Chesterfield. Probably I should be glad he was no Chesterfield because the Fourth Earl of Chesterfield behaved disreputably with women while my father's philosophy was that the best way to spend an evening is eating with a beautiful lady, drinking with a beautiful lady, and sleeping ... with a clear conscience.

Chesterfield was the eighteenth century's answer to Polonius. Courtier, ambassador, statesman, studied conversationalist, his lasting monument are his letters to Philip Dormer Stanhope, his natural son, full of shrewd observation and worldly wisdom. Virginia Woolf was a fan: 'Here is a disillusioned politician, who is prematurely aged, who has lost his office, who is losing his teeth, who, worst fate of all, is growing deafer day by day. Yet he never allows a groan to escape him. He is never dull; he is never boring; he is never slovenly. His mind is as well-groomed as his body. Never for a moment does he "welter in an easy chair".' Dr Johnson, his contemporary, was less enthusiastic: 'This man I thought had been a Lord among wits; but, I find, he is only a wit among Lords!'

On 9 October 1747 Chestefield wrote to his son, 'There is a Spanish proverb, which says very justly, Tell me who you live with, and I will tell you what you are.' Chesterfield believed that we are 'more than half what we are by imitation' and counselled his son to find the right role models and keep the best company: 'The great point is, to choose good models, and to study them with care. People insensibly contract, not only the air, the manners, and the vices, of those with whom they commonly converse, but their virtues too, and even their way of thinking.'

Chesterfield offered specific advice as well as general homilies: 'Speak elegantly, whatever language you speak in; without which, nobody will hear you with pleasure, and, consequently, you will speak to very little purpose. An agreeable and distinct elocution; without which nobody will hear you with patience; this everybody may acquire.' You won't be surprised to learn that I rather agree with that. Equally it will come as no great shock that Chesterfield and I part company on the question of laughter: 'In my mind there is nothing so illiberal and so ill-bred as audible laughter ... I am sure that since I have had the full use of my reason nobody has ever heard me laugh.'

He was hot on courtesy, and rightly. 'Good manners to those one does not love are no more a breach of truth than "your humble servant" at the bottom of a challenge is; they are universally agreed upon, and understood to be matters of course.' Politically correct or not, no harm will come if you continue to offer your seat to a lady, let others pass through the door before you, say 'please' and 'thank you' (and send thank you notes, however brief, by return), eat with your mouth closed and keep your fingernails clean. 'There is natural good breeding, which occurs to every man of common sense, and is practised by every man of common good nature.'

When it came to women Chesterfield got it all wrong. 'A man of sense only trifles with them, plays with them, humours and flatters them, as he does with a sprightly and forward child; but he neither consults them about, nor trusts them with, serious matters.' He protested that when it came to the question of religion or matrimony he would never give any advice 'because I will not have anybody's torments in this world or the next laid to my charge'. His view of women was limited ('they have, in truth, but two passions, vanity and love') and his attitude to matrimony consequently pessimistic, 'To take a wife merely as an agreeable and rational companion, will commonly be found to be a grand mistake.' Given the undeniably agreeable and all-too-rational companionship I have enjoyed over the past twenty-five years, I am more comfortable with Martin Luther's advice, 'To rise betimes and to marry young are what no man ever repents of doing.'

I am not sure if Chesterfield took a line on early rising, but he certainly favoured the industrious: 'Idleness is only the refuge of weak minds'. (Yes, but recently, I am sorry to say only relatively recently, I have begun to recognise the difference between activity and achievement. As the tycoon said, 'Don't tell me how hard you work; tell me how much you get done.') Chesterfield recognised that one needs to be a doer as much as a thinker: 'Knowledge may give weight, but accomplishments add lustre, and many more people see than weigh.' (Yes, but do not despise the intellectuals; on your own terms join them if you can; and if you can't, do not lose too much sleep. Remember Max Beerbohm's lament: 'It distresses me, this failure to keep pace with the leaders of thought, as they pass into oblivion.' Don't underestimate the man in the street; don't overestimate the senior civil servant. Reserve your awe for the Nobel prize-winners; give the rest your respect.)

Over the years plenty of worldly wisdom has come my way (don't despise your poor relations, they may become suddenly rich one day; the only way to get the best of an argument is to avoid it; he who hesitates is sometimes saved; less is more; don't ask the barber whether you need a haircut; if you want to get along, go along; think before you think; never say never; remember than one man's cliché is another man's startling *aperçu*), but for worthwhile advice from a father to a son that repays consideration you could do worse than equip yourself with a copy of Chesterfield's *Letters*.

Be wiser than other people if you can, but do not tell them so. Due attention to the inside of books, and due contempt for the outside, is the proper relation between a man of sense and his books.

Do as you would be done by is the surest method that I know of pleasing.

A man who will show every knave or fool that he thinks him such, will engage in a most ruinious war against numbers much superior to those that he and his allies can bring into the field.

There is no living in the world without a complaisant indulgence for people's weaknesses, and innocent, though ridiculous vanities. If a man has a mind to be thought wiser, and a woman handsomer than they really are, their error is a comfortable one to themselves, and an innocent one with regard to other people; and I would rather make them my friends, by indulging them in it, than my enemies, by endeavouring (and that to no purpose) to undeceive them.

The less one has to do the less time one finds to do it in.

An injury is much sooner forgotten than an insult.

Advice is seldom welcome; and those who want it the most always want it the least.

SURPRISE

'The failure is to be forty and not to have tried.'
Beatrice Colen

PG Wodehouse is a fount of sound advice. 'Never put anything on paper, my boy, and never trust a man with a small black moustache.'

Now that I have moved into the world of leak and counter-leak, the perils of committing anything to paper are borne in on me daily. In Westminster and Whitehall, the word 'Confidential' on the top of a document is almost an incitement to publish. You must not always blame the civil servants. There is the fabled occasion when the Parliamentary Under Secretary of State in the Lords dutifully read out the note on the ministerial brief, 'This is a rotten argument, but it should be good enough for their lordships on a hot summer afternoon.'

I am surprised to find that over the past quarter of a century I have earned half my living putting pen to paper and finger to key. It is not what I had expected and it might not have happened if a literary agent hadn't seen me in a televised debate from the Oxford Union and invited me up to London for lunch at the Gay Hussar in Greek Street. Over the authentic Hungarian goulash, there was no hand on knee, but there was a definite proposition. If I wanted to write, she would find me work. Her name was Irene Josephy, her rate was ten per cent, her other authors included Patrick Campbell, Angela Carter, Molly Parkin, Paul Foot. (Michael Foot was sitting at the next table.) I didn't think about it; I simply said yes. ('During the first period of a man's life the greatest danger is: *not to take the risk*.' Kierkegaard.)

I was already producing occasional articles for the teenage girls' magazine *Honey*, where I was recruited to a small band of writers who masqueraded under the soubriquet of Luke Jarvis. Luke, if you believed the editor and the photograph of the male model that accompanied his pieces, was a wise-cracking hunk of blonde manhood who boasted an Alfa Romeo, a pad in Chelsea and a string of seventeen-year-old girl-friends. In monthly instalments we chronicled his anodyne adventures, concentrating on instruction, on 'action, incident and romance with light rather than heavy petting'. With good reason, Irene felt I should be made of sterner stuff and sent me off to meet one of her other clients, a no-nonsense investigative journalist who worked for the *Sunday Times* Insight team (may even have founded it) and who lived for the hard-won exclusive exposé and the ruthless night editor's day-break call despatching him to Saigon or Santiago at a moment's notice. 'I have two bags permanently packed and waiting by the front door,' he explained, 'one for assignments above the equator, one for below.' When I revealed that I possessed just one passport (he had seven) and hadn't appreciated that the only secure place for your emergency passport is in a weatherproof pouch taped inside your car's front right-hand wing above the wheel, he dismissed me, rightly, as a journalistic milksop, fit only for features. Irene got the message and secured me a weekly column on the *Manchester Evening News*. At least the paper had a gritty editor (Brian Redhead) and in the North West I was getting back to my roots. (My maternal grandfather was living in Accrington and my father and his family were Cheshire born and bred.) I don't believe my column was any good ('Gyles Brandreth –

For the Young in Heart – Every Tuesday'), but I was earning a living and, after a fashion, learning my craft.

I needed to learn fast because journalistic greatness was about to be thrust upon me. Godfrey Winn, 'a man whose popular readership probably ranks higher than any other journalist' (*The Times*), had collapsed on the tennis court and died, aged only 64, and his weekly page in *Woman*, then the best-selling magazine of its kind on the planet earth, had fallen suddenly, unexpectedly, vacant. This was to be my glorious inheritance. I don't know where the idea originated – did my agent push me? did the magazine seek me out? – but Irene and the editor seemed to agree that I was ready to fill the great man's shoes – elegant patent leather dancing pumps, really – so after protracted negotiations, lengthy exploratory lunches, even, I recall, some trial pieces, the deal was done. The hype (an ugly but useful word that had no currency in 1972) was considerable: TV commercials, full page ads in the tabloids, a memorable photo session which included my first (and, sadly, last) encounter with a wind machine that blew through my thick hair (ah, happy days!) and was intended to transform me into a glorious amalgam of Buchan's Hannay and Brontë's Heathcliff. 'Gyles Brandreth,' ran the by-line, 'he's as modern as tomorrow with a lot of time for yesterday.'

My son, it is salutary to be introduced to failure at an early age. The column didn't work. My heart wasn't in it. That was exactly the problem. Lord Beaverbrook, a great newspaperman and his principal employer for many years, said Godfrey 'shakes hands with people's hearts'. I wasn't even on nodding acquaintance with their passing fancies. Godfrey's style was not my style; he was absurd (famously, in 1938, when the Prime Minister came back from Germany promising peace in our time, 'Praise be to God and to Mr Chamberlain. I find no sacrilege, no bathos, in coupling these two names'); he was dangerously sentimental ('If you find that your own dog doesn't take to your boy and greet him with affection, you can make up your mind on the spot that there's a yellow streak in that young man's make-up somewhere'); but he was true to himself, and his readers knew it. 'Sincerity, once you can fake that you've got it made' is a good line, but it won't wash. In journalism, in entertainment, in politics, the public wants – and knows – The Real Thing. If it's undiluted sugar they're after they won't want watered down Sweetex – and I fear my pieces weren't even as good as that.

I wasn't fired. I worked out my initial contract, starting in full colour at the front of the magazine, and gradually moving from a right-hand page to a left, then to half a page in black and white, then to the back quarter of the magazine, then to a third of a page, then out. Even the *New Statesman* recognised Godfrey Winn for what he was, 'A phenomenon, the highest-paid English journalist of his kind in history.' They were just as perceptive about me, 'His *Woman* column is very dreary stuff indeed.'

(The *New Statesman*, by the way, was a lively publication in those days. My favourite feature was the competition. I still treasure the readers' suggestions of 'Unhelpful Advice for Foreign Tourists': 'Comments from the public are always welcome in courts of law. When you start speaking, an usher will call "Silence in court" to ensure that you are heard without interruption' from Peter Alexander; 'Most foreign tourists know that in London they are encouraged to take a piece of fruit, free of charge, from any open-air stall or display' from Michael Lipton; 'On first entering an underground train, it is customary to shake hands with every passenger' from RJ Philips; 'Women are not allowed upstairs on buses; if you see a woman there ask her politely to descend' from David Gordon; and 'Try the famous echo in the British Museum Reading Room' from the incomparable Gerard Hoffnung.)

Writing my first book was a more rewarding experience. Called *Created in Captivity* it was about prisons and what, if anything, we can learn about the nature of imprisonment through the creative work of inmates (writing, painting, drama, etc) and what part, if any, that creative work can play in the process of rehabilitation. I was commissioned to write the book while I was still at university (and given an advance of £500!) but the subject had been of interest to me for a number of years and had led me to visit a wide range of penal institutions throughout Europe and North America. My research for the book had begun in a grim nineteenth-century gaol in Caen in Northern France when I was just seventeen and ended in a Soviet penitentiary just outside Moscow when I was twenty-one.

I was homesick in Russia, and frightened, which may explain why my abiding memory of Moscow is of my last night, when I went alone to see the Bolshoi Ballet who were dancing, exceptionally, not in their own theatre but in the sumptuous Palace of Congresses, a modern auditorium within the Kremlin complex. It was *Swan Lake* and it was perfect. When the interval came I needed the loo, but I had difficulty locating it because I didn't speak any Russian and they didn't have any of those convenient silhouettes on the door of men wearing kilts. After a couple of duff shots I found myself in what appeared to be the right place and locked myself in a cubicle. Moments later the bell rang for the Second Act. I made to leave, but the lock wouldn't move. I twisted it, I turned it, I tugged it, I banged at it with my shoe. It would not budge. I was locked in – locked in a Russian lavatory, a prisoner in a soviet loo, yup, I was trapped in a Commie khazi. What could I do? I banged on the door. Nobody came. I could hear the faintest strains of *Swan Lake* in the distance. I went on banging. Still no one came. There was just a tiny gap at the foot of the door, no more than an inch, a tiny gap at the top. There was no escape. I felt very bleak and more than a little alarmed, and then something curiously comforting happened that enabled me to endure the ordeal. Glancing down at the lavatory bowl, there, in the middle of the Kremlin, in the heart of the Soviet Union, at the epicentre of the Communist world, I saw the words 'Armitage Shanks'. As I waited for two long hours for the janitor to come and release me, I felt very proud to be British.

I felt proud too when *Created in Captivity* was published. If you read it now (please don't) I am sure it would seem trite and naïve, but at the time it received gratifyingly respectable reviews and sold all of 691 copies, which probably isn't too bad for a book about prison reform. The next book with which I was involved sold something like 100,000 copies – but then I wasn't the author, although for a few weeks I pretended to be ...

My publishers were also the publishers of Charles Schulz, the cartoonist of genius who created Charlie Brown and the Peanuts gang, and one day when I was in the office – no doubt discussing strategies for shifting *Created in Captivity* over the 700 mark – I asked, in passing, about the next Schulz bestseller scheduled for the list.

'It's going to be a novel by Snoopy called *It Was a Dark and Stormy Night*. It's a bit different from the usual Peanuts paperback. It's a proper book.'

'Are you planning an author tour?' I asked.

'Don't be stupid. It's supposed to be by Snoopy.'

'Exactly,' I said.

And that's how I came to spend a month of my life dressed as a seven foot beagle. Snoopy (with me inside, the unnamed man beneath the skin) began his author tour with a mock arrival at Heathrow, followed by a crowded Press Conference at the Playboy Club in Park Lane hosted by Clement Freud (not yet an MP, still a dog-food promoter). We made the front page and the early evening news (with no one calling our bluff) and then zigzagged through the United Kingdom, from Bristol to Cardiff (where the sight of this gigantic hound crossing Newport Road so startled a bus driver that he drove his vehicle into a bollard) to Liverpool, to Glasgow, to Edinburgh (where I had to walk three miles between bookshops when we discovered that Snoopy's head was too large to fit inside a black cab), to Leeds, to Manchester (where we were turned away from the French Restaurant at the Midland Hotel: 'Don't you serve dogs?' I drawled indignantly in my indifferent Californian accent; 'It's not that, sir; it's that you're not wearing a tie.') Wherever we went the crowds turned out in force and the queues at the signing sessions (where there were always more adults than children) would have made even my friend Jeffrey Archer turn green. They must have realised it was just a man in a dog suit but that didn't stop them standing in line for half an hour at a time waiting to buy the book and shake my paw.

We ended the first leg of the tour in Leicester, where the publishers had offices and had planned a Saturday morning 'Snoopy Cavalcade' in which I would be driven through the centre of the city in an open-topped bus distributing pawed photographs and promotional balloons to the multitude. I was careful never to be seen clambering into the costume and, once I was inside the skin, I stayed that way. That Saturday morning I arrived as myself and slipped discreetly into the cloakroom at the publishers to pull on my skin. I was adjusting the ears when, looking in the mirror, I realised that behind me there was a figure lurking furtively in one of the cubicles. I turned slowly round and pushed the cubicle door ajar. Standing there, in the full uniform of a cub scout Akela, was a woman who was as startled as I was. 'Who are you? What are you doing in the Ladies?' she asked.

'I'm so sorry,' I stammered, 'I didn't realise. I was sent in here to change. Who are you?'

'I'm Jane,' she said, 'I work here.'

'Oh,' I found myself saying, 'me Snoopy, you Jane.'

She turned out to be the publisher's children's editor based in Leicester and the unexpeced encounter changed my life. Before the day was done, and believe it or not, before I had taken off Snoopy's head to reveal my own, she had asked me to write a book. In the end I wrote twenty or more for her and began an involvement in children's books, as a writer and publisher, that has gone on ever since. If I hadn't spent that month as Snoopy it might never have happened.

And that's the moral of the story. If now and again you do something surprising something surprising can happen to you. Noël Coward's advice to David Lean was 'keep coming out of a different hole'. I would add to that, don't simply surprise others, surprise yourself. Once in a while surprise yourself with what you eat and what you wear and what you read and where you go. I knew I would like Venice: I had no idea how much I would like pony-trekking in Iceland. Surprise yourself by what you latch on to, surprise yourself by letting go. (For ten years we owned a wonderful painting by Laura Knight, a scene of a curtain call at the ballet viewed from the flies. It was my favourite picture. I loved it. I looked at it with pleasure every day. Then we sold it. I let go and found it didn't hurt at all. It was only a picture and I felt suddenly quite free.) Most of all try to surprise yourself in the way you think. I remember being entertained by Edward de Bono at the Athenaeum in Pall Mall ('A memory is what is left when something happens and does not completely unhappen' *The Mechanism of Mind*) and coming away startled and exhilarated by his clarion call: Think sideways.

As a politician you can be sure I am not advocating perpetual revolution, never-ending change, upheaval for its own sake, but as a father and friend, I do recommend that, now and again, you allow into every aspect of your life the element of surprise. As I was saying, PG Wodehouse is a fount of sound advice: 'I don't know if you have ever leaped between the sheets, all ready for a spot of sleep, and received an unforeseen lizard up the left pyjama leg? It's an experience which puts its stamp on a man.'

TELEVISION

'In my experience, television is for appearing on, not looking at.'
Noël Coward

The great Richard Cobb, Professor of Modern History at the University of Oxford and celebrated author of *Les armées révolutionnaires*, taught me what little I know about the French Revolution. I was fortunate to have him as my tutor, not simply because he was the world authority on the subject, but because he was then at Balliol and I was at New College. His fearsome reputation, both as intellectual and eccentric, ensured that I turned up for my first tutorial a minute or two early and in a state of some trepidation. Deliberately I paced myself as I clambered the stairs to his room. I stood outside his door, waiting for the clock in the quadrangle to strike four, wondering if he would prove to be as alarming as I had been led to believe. As the clock began to strike and I raised my hand to knock, from within the room, I heard him.

'What the bloody hell have you done with it?' he was shouting. 'Damn and blast your eyes! Where the hell is it?'

I knew he wrote his history in fluent French. He appeared to approach his pupils in the vernacular.

'You are so bloody – bloody – *bloody* stupid!' His rage was mounting.

'For Chrissake, where have you put it? God how I despise

you!' He paused. 'And where the hell's my next pupil?'

This was my cue to knock, but given the way he appeared to be berating his current pupil I was not over-eager to be next in the firing line.

'Bloody hell!' Suddenly I heard a crash. It sounded as though he had heaved a pile of books onto the floor. Then the voice rose to a crescendo of fury. 'Where the fuck is he?'

It was three minutes past four. I knocked.

'Come!'

I turned the handle, pushed open the door and found him standing in the middle of his study, wild-eyed, hair dishevelled, books and papers littered pell-mell on the floor around him. He appeared to be alone. There was a door beyond him that led, presumably, to his bedroom. Had the other pupil taken refuge in there?

'Ah, yes, good ... ' he mumbled, beckoning me into the room. 'You must be, er ...'

'Brandreth, yes. Am I disturbing you?'

'No, no. Find a seat. Move those books. I was expecting you. You're late.'

'I'm sorry,' I faltered. 'I thought you had someone with you.'

'No, no. I was talking to myself. I couldn't find a document I needed. Now what did you say your name was?'

'Brandreth.'

'Oh,' he smiled. ' "The television star". Shall we have a glass of wine?'

At this stage the 'television star' had made a grand total of five appearances on the small screen. In the first I had been interviewed by Robin Day (bow-ties were his jumpers) for the BBC's *Panorama*. Roy Jenkins was moving from the Home Office to the Treasury and being tipped for the top. What did the younger generation make of him? Next came Ken Tynan's documentary and a similar exercise for West German TV ('*Hier ist das guldenes Jugend aus Oxford ...*'). And, finally, two debates broadcast live from the Union. In the first I was the undergraduate support speaker to Norman St John Stevas, and serious. In the second I was the support speaker to Frank Muir, and flippant. In both I was noticeable, irritating, probably, to my contemporaries; an object of curiosity, apparently, to my elders.

I had assumed Cobb had been mocking me when he dubbed me the television star. I was wrong. He was teasing, certainly, but not scornful. Oddly, for one so intellectually gifted and acclaimed, he was drawn to pupils who had rather more superficial attributes. He seemed especially taken with young aristocrats, the older the title, the fuller the entry in Debrett's, the more stately the ancestral pile, the better. Cobb took a keen interest in my burgeoning television career and seemed genuinely concerned that my studies shouldn't get in the way of it.

In the Michaelmas term of my Finals year (the autumn of 1969) I was engaged to script and host ITV's farewell to the passing decade. The show was called *A Child of the Sixties* (I was the child), the producer a veteran of such distinguished productions as *The World at War* and *The Life and Times of Lord Mountbatten*, and the production based at London Weekend's studios at Wembley, whence I had to go for regular script conferences throughout the term. I had no difficulty juggling these with my tutorials because Richard Cobb proposed that we should travel up to London together on the train. From Oxford to Didcot we would gossip, then, fortified with a paper cup or two of BR *vin ordinaire*, the great man would do his best to help me get to grips with the fiscal disorders of the *Ancien Régime*.

The reception accorded to *A Child of the Sixties* ('Suddenly a new Frost is born') led me to think that perhaps I was going to be rich and famous sooner rather than later. 'Gyles is the 21-year-old student who appeared on the London Weekend look-back programme on Saturday and was told afterwards, "You can write your own ticket in TV now." ' It didn't turn out quite that way. Was it Cyril

Connolly who said, 'Those whom the gods wish to destroy they first call promising'? (Or was it John Moore?) The programme produced a spate of features, but no overnight stardom. I pasted the cuttings into my scrapbook and reverted to tutorials at New College and Balliol rather than Didcot, Reading and Paddington. The last day of my Finals coincided with the General Election at which Edward Heath became Prime Minister, and I was on hand to give Robin Day (and the nation) my reaction to the momentous event. (The other side of the story was put by Jack Straw, then President of the National Union of Students.) When I left Oxford in the summer of 1970 I reckoned that broadcasting would be part of my life, but only part of it.

My first post-graduate TV assignment was a documentary entitled *The Saint and the Cynic.* The Saint was Thomas à Becket, the eight-hundredth anniversary of whose martyrdom was the peg for the film, in which I was supposed to play the cynic and cross-question the present Archbishop of Canterbury, everybody's favourite uncle, the prelate with the eyebrows and the twinkle, Michael Ramsey. Music was to be provided by Yehudi Menuhin, playing unaccompanied Bach on the very spot where the four knights, Reginald Fitzurse, William de Tracy, Hugh de Merville and Richard de Breton, had cut down the turbulent priest in 1170.

In my experience, most television is about as memorable to be in as it is to watch, but an incident occurred during our filming at Canterbury Cathedral that I have not forgotten. The Archbishop and I were standing at the top of the steps leading down to the crypt when Yehudi Menuhin arrived and I was startled to find that he had his violin case handcuffed to his wrist.

'For the insurance people,' he explained. 'It is a very valuable instrument, a Stradivarius.'

'Oh, how exciting,' I exclaimed, as Menuhin unlocked the handcuff, opened the case and, with appropriate veneration and care, took out his violin.

'It – is – *beautiful*!' I gushed.

'Certainly, it has a beautiful tone,' said Menuhin.

'May I hold it a moment?' I asked.

'By all means,' said Menuhin, 'but be careful.' He handed me the precious instrument. I took it with both hands.

'My, my,' I murmured appreciatively. 'Have you seen this, Your Grace?' I said to the Archbishop, who was standing a few steps away from me. 'To think I am holding Yehudi Menuhin's Stradivarius!' I must have turned to face Dr Ramsey with a touch too much youthful exuberance, because, as I turned, the instrument flew swiftly and easily out of my hands. I made to catch it and, as I did so, tilted the edge and sent it spinning gracefully towards the crypt. It bounced its way elegantly – and audibly – down the ancient stone stairway and landed, with a crash, all strings broken, at the foot of the steps, about a yard from the very spot where Becket was murdered.

Menuhin's many years of meditation had been but a preparation for this moment in his life. He did not offer a word of reproach. He closed his eyes for a second and took a deep and deliberate breath. Then, quite calmly, he walked down the stone steps to retrieve his bruised Stradivarius. Carefully, he inspected the instrument.

'I think I'll have to use the other one,' he said with a modest shrug. (So this was the secret of his serenity: meditation, macrobiotics and a spare Strad in the boot.)

'You have another violin with you then?'

'Yes,' he said, 'it's in the car.'

'Let me get it for you,' I volunteered.

Briefly his face did seem to twitch. 'Er, no, I'll fetch it myself. Thank you all the same.'

In the dozen or so years that followed I earned perhaps half my living from broadcasting, but because I never took it quite seriously it never took me quite seriously. I did radio: panel games, a bit of disc jockeying, the occasional documentary. In television I worked on scores of programmes, straight and light, on camera and off (I have specially happy memories of scripting three series of a sitcom called *Dear Ladies* for Hinge and Bracket), but quite quickly I found I had drifted into the twilight zone of the game show. I devised one or two (the best was *The Railway Carriage Game* – nice idea – deserves a revival – Chris Evans as host?), worked behind the scenes on several more (the worst – though I had a happy time working on it – was a Japanese import, renamed *Ultra Quiz*, which we emasculated and the public shunned) and appeared in hundreds as a casual member of an informal repertory company of game show guests ('another studio, another jumper'). I enjoyed the money (travelling in a lift with Bruce Forsyth at LWT one day I said to him, 'Isn't it marvellous, I'm going to do two shows this evening and I'll earn £400.' 'Yeah, luv,' said Brucie. 'It's great. I'm going to do two shows too and I'll earn £16,000.'), I liked the people, and the triviality of it didn't trouble me because it was only a slice of life and, for me, a fairly slim slice at that.

In 1983 breakfast television came to Britain. I watched the dawning of TV-am from a hotel bedroom in Manchester. I set the alarm for 5.59 am so that I could witness this little bit of television history from the start. I am afraid I didn't stay the course. The programme began with a magisterial presentation of the news from BAFTA award-winning Robert Kee that seemed to go on and on – and on – until the switch went off and my head fell back on the pillow. Apparently, I was not alone.

TV-am, despite the hype, despite the high-profile presenters (or, rather, in part because of them) turned out to be an instant flop. The audience began small and became smaller. By the time Greg Dyke was brought in from London Weekend to salvage the wreck I believe the viewers were so few that they didn't even register on the ratings. Gradually Greg transformed the show. The old presenters disappeared – much crying over spilt wine – to be replaced by Anne and

Nick, unknown but so likeable, the idealised couple next
door, supported by a mixed bag of characters like Diana
Dors and Jimmy Greaves, and, most sensationally, Roland,
the only rat famous for climbing aboard a sinking ship. Greg
saved the station by giving his viewers what they wanted
rather than what the great and the good of the telly
establishment might feel was good for them. The formula
was simple: bright and breezy, light then shade then light
again, nothing longer than three minutes, nothing too heavy
('It's six o'clock in the bleeding morning, for Christ's sake! '
G Dyke, 1983) and a cast of free and easy folk on the sofa
who were there to befriend not threaten. It worked in very
much the same way as the BBC's *Tonight* programme
worked in the late fifties and early sixties. Variations in the
formula were imperceptible and the presenters weren't
offered to you as individuals, but as members of a family,
almost like characters in an uncontroversial soap opera, with
a rock solid couple at the centre and one or two loveable
eccentrics among the siblings and cousins and uncles and
aunts.

I had worked occasionally for Greg on the *Six O'Clock
Show* at London Weekend and it was a lucky day for me
when, in that summer of 1983, he asked me to join the gang.
I stayed with TV-am for seven years, initially doing one
morning a week, eventually doing three or four. It was a
happy time. It was gratifying to be earning good money
before breakfast, and there was the bonus of an endless series
of intriguing brief encounters. In the eighties 'everybody
who is anybody' touched base with the TV-am sofa.
Sylvester Stallone was shorter than I expected, Joan Collins
gentler and prettier. Peter Ustinov was wonderfully droll (at
7.15 am!), Anthony Hopkins was even funnier (but not on
the sofa, in the canteen afterwards, doing the best Olivier
impressions I've heard). There was a palpable aura about
Billy Graham (probably the encounter that impressed me
most) and a menacing posse around Jesse Jackson (just

security men, but they kept their man encircled at all times. It was the same with Eddie Murphy: to have a conversation you had to shout across a human barricade of guards.) We met heroes and superstars, some humble, some less so. Willy Brandt was delightfully unassuming for a former West German Chancellor: 'Just call me Willy.' I sat down on the sofa next to Charlton Heston and put my mug of tea on the table in front of us. Immediately he picked it up and began sipping from it. When you are a star I suppose you take it for granted that any refreshment brought into your presence must be for you.

Greg Dyke saved TV-am. Bruce Gyngell, who replaced him quite quickly, sustained the success and turned the company into a worthwhile business. For me, the foul-mouthed Dyke had a lot of charm and the smooth-talking Australian Gyngell very little. I warmed to his achievement, but his personality left me cold. He made great play of his affability and approachability, but most of the team seemed to find him quite frightening. The line was, 'When Bruce says "G'day, sit down!" you don't bother to look for a chair.' We all recognised that he knew what he was doing. His obsession with the colour pink was totally valid. Light, bright colours make you feel good. Who wants to have some old buffer giving you the weather when you can wake up with Ulrika Jonsson? He fired the lady who persisted in appearing in black. 'We're the sunshine station dammit.' He was tough, arrogant, committed, a magnificent leader during the strike that freed British commercial television from the shackles of the old-style unions, but when TV-am failed to regain its franchise I thought of Bruce and the words *hubris* and *nemesis* came to mind.

My happiest times at the station were in the very early days, when we had no audience, our backs to the wall and a real spirit of adventure, and towards the very end, in the summer of 1990, when Anne Diamond replaced David Frost on Sunday mornings and I was her side-kick. It was one of

my last Sundays with the station when Edward Fox and
David Owen were the guests. We invited them to join us in
'test-tasting' the new range of British Rail sandwiches
designed by Clement Freud. (I remember thinking, Gerald du
Maurier lent his name to cigarettes, Elizabeth Taylor lends
hers to perfume, and Clement Freud ends up with BR
sandwiches. Is this life after politics? After Liberal politics,
possibly ...). Rex Harrison had died the night before, and
since Edward Fox had recently been appearing with him in
The Admirable Crichton, Anne turned to him for some
appropriate actor-laddie reminiscences.

Anne: Did you know Rex Harrison?
Edward: Yes.
Anne: Did you like him?
Edward: Yes. Ver' much.
Anne: What was he like?
Edward: Erm ... er ... a genius.
Anne: What kind of genius?
Edward: (PAUSE) A genius.
Anne: But how did the genius manifest itself?
Edward: (PAUSE) Either the sun shines or it doesn't.
Anne: He was very much a stage actor?
Edward: Yes.
Anne: And films?
Edward: Yes.

I wondered, is Edward related to the Queen after all?

Afterwards, we joined Dr Owen for breakfast in the
canteen. It was the day that he and his SDP colleagues were
to get together to decide whether or not to disband their
party in the wake of the Bootle by-election where the Social
Democrat candidate fared rather worse than the Monster
Raving Loony. Owen told us that, while his party might now
be dismissed as a joke, he believed he still had credibility. He
quoted a couple of opinion polls showing that the public
would rather have him as Prime Minister than either

Margaret Thatcher or Neil Kinnock. He prophesied that the general election would be very close, with Thatcher the victor by a narrow margin ('They vote for her hating her because they know where she stands') and his hope was that in the run-up to the election the polls would show it to be so close that Kinnock would turn to him to deliver key votes in key marginals. He would stand out for a few concessions – the Scottish Assembly, proportional representation in the Euro-elections – and in the event of a narrow Labour victory could see himself as a possible Foreign Secretary. 'It can't be Kaufman. Kinnock would do better to bring Healey out of retirement for a couple of years.' He wasn't bothered that Kinnock was no intellectual titan. 'He'll manage the party and the civil servants can run the country.' He ate an orange for breakfast and then went out into the forecourt where half of Fleet Street was waiting to photograph him.

I poured another cup of coffee and thought, 'If I don't stand in this election, I'm going to have to wait another five years.' In politics, as in war, and much else besides, timing is everything. Always remember the famous last words of General Sedgwick at the Battle of Spotsylvania: 'They couldn't hit an elephant at this dist—'

VOTES

'Wednesday, 31st December 1969

This Christmas and New Year there have been a whole series of
television programmes looking back not only at 1969 but at the
whole decade. I saw one which had the President of the Oxford
Union, a young Tory, handsome, good-looking, waving his delicate
fingers about as he sat on a dais and put questions – this is the
strange thing – to Michael Foot, Elizabeth Longford, Iain Macleod
and Alf Friendly. The idea was to see the 1960s through the eyes of
a child of the decade, someone who had grown up in the age of
television. This young man had no ideas or ideals. He just shared
the general disillusionment and all his illustrations of the decade
were public occasions in the newsreels, Vietnam, the murder of
Jack Kennedy, the murder of Robert Kennedy, of Martin Luther
King, everything that obviously illustrated the 1960s as a period of
degeneration, decline, disappointment, lack of hope, deflation. This
young man didn't stand for anything. Michael struggled with him
from his elderly position. Elizabeth, in her own Catholic style,
stood for something, and even Iain Macleod did but it was an
extremely depressing programme. Not only were they being
cross-examined by this young pup, but they fawned on him, all
saying, "It's you that matters, your ideals, your beliefs." '

Richard Crossman, *The Diaries of a Cabinet Minister*

Crossman was wrong in more than one respect. I had ideals
and I had ideas. Indeed, I had more than ideas. I had the
answers – all of them. From the restructuring of the prison
system to the introduction of national community service for
all school-leavers, from equal opportunities legislation to

wholesale tax reform, I had a complete programme ready for implementation. Since around the time of the 1959 General Election I had assumed that mine would be a life in politics. By 1969 I was ready to take the first step.

I am not sure if people have political heroes nowadays, but when I was your age, Iain Macleod was mine. One of R A Butler's team at the Conservative Research Department after the War, Minister of Health then Minister of Labour in the fifties, Colonial Secretary overseeing 'the end of Empire' at the start of the sixties, he became Chancellor of the Exchequer in June 1970 and died after only a matter of weeks in office, aged 56. He was a One Nation Tory, who liked to quote Disraeli, yet had the gift of making the difficult seem easy, the complex clear. He was ready for the muck and bullets of parliamentary warfare – with a mordant wit and withering debating style – but he could also lift your eyes to the shining castle on the hill. Jeremiah Brandreth, a Luddite accused of leading an insurrection against the government in 1817 and consequently the last person to be beheaded for treason in England, was known as 'the hopeless radical'. I saw myself as the hopeful radical and Macleod was my role model.

When I had invited him to come and speak at the Union he had declined ('I grow old, I grow old, and apart from keeping my trousers rolled, I have given up university debating'), but he had given me an interview for the *Oxford Tory* and at our preparatory meetings in the run-up to making *A Child of the Sixties* he had given me time and kindly attention way beyond my desserts. He made a conscious effort (and not just when he was Chairman of the Party) to woo and win the hearts and minds of young people. With me, and thousands like me, he succeeded.

And now, here he was, 'a guest on my show'. The opportunity was too good to miss. In politics, after all, timing is everything. After the recording, over drinks in the hospitality suite, I took my courage in my hands and approached him with a directness that I am alarmed to recollect: 'Mr Macleod, I am hoping to become a member of parliament. I wonder if you can help?' He turned his stooped shoulders towards me and raised an eyebrow. I imagine I hoped he would put an avuncular arm around my shoulder and lead me off into a corner to discuss which safe seat I should try for first. In fact he said, 'Young man,' and while the tone was friendly, already I could tell that what was to follow would be disconcerting, 'You may think you know it all, but you've probably got a little to learn yet. I suggest you find yourself a wife. She'll teach you a thing or two. Have some children. They'll knock the stuffing out of you. Get yourself a job, have a career, build a business, make something, do something, be something. Then come and see me.' He smiled and turned back to finish his conversation with Michael Foot.

That I took Macleod's advice was not entirely due to him. When we married Michèle made me promise not to pursue my political ambitions until our children were teenagers. She sensed that politics and young families don't mix. (Having now experienced the lunatic routine at Westminster, it turns out she was right about that, as well as everything else.) When, eventually, I did set out to become an MP, twenty years after *A Child of the Sixties*, it was the year our youngest daughter turned thirteen (is this a politician who keeps his promises?) and I found, though I had not given the matter much conscious thought, that what motivated me in 1990 was rather different from what had motivated me in 1969. At 21, it was the cut and thrust of the political debate that I found exhilarating, the arguments, the point-scoring, no doubt, too, I am afraid, the sound of my own voice. At 42, while still ready for the argy-bargy of political warfare, I saw it as a means not as an end. Anyone can make a noise, the trick is to make a difference. When Iain Macleod, master of the combative arts, arrived at the Treasury he told his officials, 'Whatever I may have said in Opposition, I am not interested in opposition. I am interested in administration.'

What interested me was the detail of administration, the mechanism of government, the machinery and what makes it tick, and how you can tweak it to achieve your ends. I had always enjoyed the game of politics. I had long been fascinated by 'the art of the possible', the secret of leading while taking people with you, the inspirational management of change, the harnessing of the political will. Now I wanted to see as well what difference an individual might be able to make, not in any grandiose way, not on a grand scale, but in small ways, as an ordinary backbencher, simply working the system. I no longer had all the answers, but somewhere along the line I had come across William Blake's dictum that 'he who would do good must do it by minute particulars'.

I said goodbye to TV-am and went on a happy holiday to Verona. The day I got back, at the beginning of September 1990, I wrote to Sir Tom Arnold MP, Vice-Chairman of the Conservative Party in charge of candidates, explaining that my services were now to be at the disposal of the Party and the nation and requesting an audience to discuss the matter further. A secretary acknowledged my communication and I was invited to attend an interview at 3.20 pm on 5 November. (My boy, when it is the secretary who gets in touch, when the appointment is two months' hence, and when the time offered is twenty past or twenty to, you can be fairly sure you are not high on the list of priorities....) On the due day I presented myself at Central Office where I was ushered past a magnificent portrait of Margaret Thatcher in the foyer, up what felt very much like the back stairs, and into a tiny office where I found Sir Tom sitting behind a small, sparsely covered desk, exuding the discreet charm of the seasoned Tory MP. We exchanged pleasantries and then I came to the point. Could I join the candidates list? Sir Tom was cordial but non-committal. Officially, the list was now closed, but here were the forms and if I cared to fill them in and could find appropriate sponsors we'd take it from there. Would, let's look in the diary, 19 December at 6.30 pm be convenient for a further meeting? (I knew that at 6.30 pm on 19 December I would be on stage with Barbara Windsor at the Wimbledon Theatre, half-way through the dress rehearsal for *Cinderella*, but all the same I said Yes. Timing is everything.) I was out by three-thirty, the conversation had been brief and straightforward, but the combination of Tom's manner – a hushed tone, a certain urgency of delivery, a face with a touch of sadness in repose transformed by sudden brilliant smiles – and the smallness of the room gave the encounter an oddly conspiratorial quality. At Oxford I had always felt hurt that no one had approached me about the possibility of joining MI6. I imagined the initial interview would have felt like this.

At 6.00 pm on 19 December the gods smiled on Wimbledon and the producer announced the supper-break. 'Back at seven, sharp!' I tore off my Baron Hardup costume, threw on my charcoal grey suit, leapt into the waiting cab and arrived at Smith Square at 6.20 pm. I was ushered past a magnificent portrait of John Major in the foyer (a month is a long time in politics) and at 6.30 pm found myself once again closeted with Sir Tom. I handed over the completed forms. Mmm ... mmm ... very good ... mmm ... yes ... fine. I asked the question I needed to ask (always remember, my boy, when you go into a meeting what you hope to get out of it): 'I appreciate I'm not yet on the list, but, while you're processing this, if a possibility crops up, would it be okay for me to throw my hat into the ring?' Mmm ... mmm ... I don't see why not. At 7.03 pm, on the stage of the Wimbledon Theatre the Lord Chamberlain (Ed 'Stewpot' Stewart) announced, 'His Excellency the Baron Hardup of Hardup Hall', and I stumbled down the stairway into Prince Charming's Palace, arriving at the Ball in the nick of time. I hadn't made it back into my costume, so the Ugly Sisters had a lot of fun with the charcoal grey suit.

Early in the New Year I read in *The Times* that Sir Peter Morrison, a former Minister of State and, until her downfall,

Mrs Thatcher's parliamentary private secretary, was planning to retire as the MP for the City of Chester at the forthcoming general election. Instantly I thought, that's the seat for me. My father was born in Cheshire, I had family from that part of the world, I knew that an MP has to sing the praises of his constituency, which might call for poetic licence in Bootle or Bridgend, but could be done *con brio* hand on heart in the case of Chester. This was a beautiful historic city, somewhere I would willingly live, its economic mix was one for which I sensed I would have a feeling and a real understanding. I went for it. Along with some two hundred and thirty other hopefuls I sent my c.v. in to the local Association Chairman. I was one of two dozen chosen for the initial interview. We were each required to give a fifteen-minute speech, without notes, on why we wanted to be the member of parliament for the City of Chester. This was followed by questions from the fourteen-strong interview panel. Having studied your mother's book, *How to Interview and be Interviewed,* I did my best to 'walk in like a winner' ('if you don't feel it, act it') and remember the five c's: be clear, concise, courteous, confident, committed. I also asked to be seen last. When interviewers are faced with a weekend of unfamiliar faces coming at them on the hour every hour, the last they see may manage to make a greater impact simply by virtue of positioning.

A week later I was back for the second interview (detailed policy now) and the notorious 'drinks party' where you and your spouse, and the other candidates and theirs, try to be affable without being forward, and, above all else, try not to spill your orange juice over the chairman's wife.

For the third and final interview the candidates had been whittled down to three in number and the selection committee had grown to one hundred. A fifteen-minute speech, half an hour of questions, then a vote. 'I am afraid you can't be last on this time, Mr Brandreth. We've drawn lots. You're first.' I did my stuff. The speech was competent, the answers to the questions less so. There was one where I didn't begin to understand what I was being asked, let alone have a clue what the informed answer should be. 'I don't know the answer to that, sir,' I said, 'but this much I promise you: I'll find out.' Applause. (My boy, it's a trick only to be used in the direst emergency; and remember, it only works once.)

By about ten o'clock it was all over. The votes had been counted. I had won. The final hurdle, the official adoption meeting the following evening at which all members of the Association would have a vote, was now to be a formality. I was the executive's sole recommendation as prospective parliamentary candidate. The challenge at the adoption meeting wasn't so much the questions as the fact that I was seated between the then President of the Association, His Grace the Duke of Westminster, and the then MP, the Rt Hon Sir Peter Morrison, both unstoppable smokers, and as the plumes of their cigarette smoke wafted up to the left and the right of me and hit my contact lenses I found that I was concluding my speech with eyes brimming with tears. Perhaps that explains the warmth of the ovation.

The Conservatives of Chester chose me as their prospective candidate on the strength of three fifteen-minute speeches, two hours of cross-questioning and a drinks party at which I reckon my wife did rather better than pass muster. A little to my surprise, and certainly to my relief, the reputation of 'the man in the woolly jumpers' did not appear to have stood in my way. Most of them had never seen me on TV and the issue was raised only once, and briefly, in the first or second interview. 'Mr Brandreth, do you think your television image will be a barrier to being taken seriously as a politician?' I had prepared an answer: 'I hope it will prove to be a bridge rather than a barrier. Most people in most parts of the country can't name their MP let alone tell you what he or she looks like. If I am a familiar face to some people in the constituency that may help make me more accessible. If I am more accessible I am more accountable.' It may have been a bit too pat, but I believed it then and I think it has proved to be true.

Clearly I was someone's idea of a good candidate. But would I be a good MP? Would I be an MP at all? This, after all, was a critical marginal, worse, a critical marginal we were predicted to lose. Indeed on the day of the election I assumed we had lost. The newspapers said as much. When I checked the television before leaving home for the count, the BBC's close of poll survey readied me for the worst. I prepared the brave face and the few gracious-words-in-defeat as Michèle and I stood around in the Town Hall watching the boxes of votes arriving and being emptied out onto the tables. Mankind might be able to send missions to Mars, but in a parliamentary democracy the votes are still counted by hand, bundled together with clothes pegs and set out on trestle tables so that you can see the pile for each candidate growing (or not) as the count proceeds. It was a close run thing, but by 2.15 am it was clear: I had won with a majority of 1,101.

There were two factors that contributed to my success. One was my local team: indefatigable, indomitable, unbeatable – efficient. (My boy, it would be politic to say this whatever the case. As it happens, it is true.) The other was the Prime Minister, who kept his head when all about were losing theirs and stood on his soapbox in the centre of Chester in the pouring rain. (It is politic to say this as well. It also happens to be true.) The last politican to travel round the country with a soapbox was George Brown in 1970. At the time people said it was the end of an era, that in the television age we wouldn't see that kind of electioneering again. 'Don't you believe it,' said George, 'elections can't just be won with set-piece rallies and in the TV studio. You've got to get out on the town hall steps, onto the street corners, let them see what you're really made of.' It worked.

WESTMINSTER

'To the young members of parliament who have just come I would say that, for the first six months after you are here, you will wonder how you got here. After that you will wonder how the rest of the members ever got here.'

John Diefenbaker

You can't beat the cliché. They said it would be like going back to school and it was.

On 9 April 1992 I joined 140 other new boys and girls at the House of Commons, a co-educational establishment for 651 students of markedly mixed abilities, set in a splendid old building on the banks of the Thames. For the first time in thirty years I felt I was wearing short trousers again.

The school begins by teaching you that, however much you may have seen yourself as the man of the match back in the constituency, here at Westminster, quite properly, the new boy is very much least among equals. You thought you knew it all. The prefects (termed 'Whips' in the traditional school slang) quickly awaken you to the fact that you don't know much.

Initially the main thing you don't know is where you are. This is hardly surprising since the Palace of Westminster boasts a thousand doors, a hundred staircases, five kilometres of corridors, but, apparently, no map. Right at the beginning of term, searching for a loo, I found myself by a door marked 'Peers Only' and decided that I was in the wrong place. A passing Old Boy (Lord Harmar-Nicholls, I think) put me on the right track by pointing out that you don't need a map when the whole place is colour-coded. Look at the carpet, look at the upholstery, look at the leather on the chairs. If they are green, you are in the Commons. If they are red, you are in the Lords. 'We don't have too many signs,' said his Lordship, 'because some of the people in our place can no longer read and we're not entirely sure if some of the people in your place ever could.'

For any other job today some qualifications would be required: NVQs perhaps, a few GCSEs, maybe an A-Level or two, even a degree. Not so at Westminster. No qualifications are necessary and no training is offered. ('What do we do with the people who have no qualifications and absolutely no training?' asks the cynic. 'We put them in charge of running the country, and then wonder why things turn out the way they do....') There is no job specification provided for new MPs, no book of rules outlining the basics either – like how to find your way in. I knew there was a Members' Entrance somewhere (I had read about it in Trollope) but it took me three days to pluck up the courage to ask a policeman where it was. 'Across that courtyard on the right, Sir, where Mr Coe is jogging in.'

Having discovered the Members' Entrance, just inside it I came across the members' cloakroom and there I found my own, my very own, personalised coat hanger. There are 651 members of parliament and consequently 651 coat hangers in the members' cloakroom, each with his or her Member's name inscribed beside it in elegant italic. Individually attached to each coat hanger is a neatly-tied loop of pink ribbon.

'It's very fetching,' I said to the policeman, 'but what's it for?'

'You don't know, sir. Really?'

'No, I'm afraid not. I'm one of the new boys.'

'Of course, sir. Well, the pink ribbon ... that's, er, where you hang your sword.'

It seems that students are not encouraged to take their swords into class. Indeed we are expected to come to school totally unarmed. That's why we never shake hands with one another. As anyone with even a glancing familiarity with the history of chivalry knows full well (but the ignorant MP for the City of Chester discovered from the Under Secretary of State for Northern Ireland on Day Two) the handshake is a medieval invention designed to prove that your hand does not conceal a weapon. As Honourable Members of the mother of parliaments that can be taken for granted with us.

Or can it? In the Chamber – where Matron presides over the daily meetings of the Debating Society – there is a thin red line woven into the green carpet in front of the benches and tradition has it that you must not step over the line when addressing the House. (You wondered about the origin of the expression 'toeing the line'? Now you know.) The distance between the two red lines is significant. During the debates the two sides are to be kept at least a double rapier length apart.

Sword-fighting is taboo. Back-stabbing is quite another matter. Within days four separate old hands had reminded this new boy of Sir Winston Churchill's celebrated dictum: 'Never confuse the Opposition with the enemy. The Opposition are the members of parliament sitting on the benches facing you. The enemy are the members of parliament sitting on the benches behind you.' As the Opposition wasn't much in evidence during my first term, the field was rather left to the enemy, with older boys leading younger ones astray, taking them behind the bicycle sheds and introducing them to unnatural non-European practices. Some blamed the new head for this. They said he was too decent for his own good. Apparently, when his predecessor raised her voice and twitched her cane, the tea room trembled. Many of the older boys seem to appreciate the more relaxed atmosphere that the Major-style has brought to Westminster. Inevitably a couple of dozen have taken advantage of it and, with a majority of nineteen, it is a couple of dozen you have to reckon with.

Understandably, some students are still wistful about the passing of the old head. She is rightly revered for her colossal achievements – there's talk of a statue somewhere in the school grounds – but when she came back half-way through term and made a lot of noise no one took much notice. She may have misjudged the date. It wasn't quite Founder's Day, but it happened to be the 89th birthday of Lord Home of the Hirsel, for most people (including Baroness Thatcher until recently) the perfect role model for all former Prime Ministers.

Most of the beaks have gone out of their way to give the impression that they take the new intake seriously, which is very decent of them. I am surprised by how much I like the other new boys and girls: they are a convivial crowd, interesting and entertaining, even if one or two of them aren't accustomed to playing team games. While the school can tolerate the occasional maverick on the wing, clearly the only way to keep winning the prizes is to play as a team.

At least the school rebels stand up to be counted. Identifying the school sneaks isn't so easy. I went to my first tutorial with the head of maths (aka 'New members briefing with the Chancellor of the Exchequer') and twenty-four hours later read a highly partial account of the meeting in *The Times*. Selective leaking and peddling a particular line in the lobby are old school traditions, but seasoned students are concerned that the growth in the indiscretion industry may lead to an unwillingness by teachers to take pupils into their confidence.

Westminster is a place where you are left to find your own feet, as well as your own place in the Chamber. By tradition the front two benches on the government's side are reserved for ministers, but you can sit anywhere else you like. To bag a place you turn up at any time from 8.00 am and position a green 'Prayer Card' with your name on it on the seat you want. If at 2.30 pm prompt (2.31 pm is too late) you return to your place for Prayers, your seat is then reserved for you for the rest of the day. During Prayers, conducted by the school chaplain, so that we do not have to eyeball our opponents across the floor of the House, we turn in our places and face the wall. A loud-mouthed fourth former called Skinner (who I rather like) is the only member who refuses to stand during Prayers. He sits in his place, arms and legs crossed, in angry agnostic defiance.

I have not seen Skinner in the Members' Dining Room, but finding your place in there takes some getting used to as well. Conservative members all sit at one end of the dining room, Labour members all sit at the other, and the Liberals wait at table. (Only teasing: the Lib-Dems have a table of their own in the middle.) Sebastian Coe and I decided to brave the dining room together on our first night. All the tables were taken, apart from one in the corner by the window. We sat ourselves down and waited. Quite some minutes later a waiter approached us and murmured, 'I take it, gentlemen, you are dining with the Chief Whip.' We didn't know, but now we do.

It takes a little time to come to terms with the realities of life as a member of parliament. In the constituency you have to adjust to the harsh fact that the MP is no longer the venerated local dignitary he might once have been. He is a curious (and preferably inexhaustible) creature who combines the skills of a social worker, Relate counsellor, Citizens' Advice Bureau, housing officer, and political punchbag, with an apparently insatiable appetite for finger food and an unquenchable desire to buy raffle tickets at every available opportunity. At Westminster you have to adjust yourself to strange hours (the average time for going home since my arrival has been midnight), to bizarre customs ('The one sure way to be called by the Speaker is to slip her a tenner, discreetly concealed in an order paper ... '. An old joke of A P Herbert's), to new disciplines ('When there is a three-line whip you will be here to vote unless you can produce a doctor's certificate ... showing you are dead.' No joke at all.)

For all the absurdities and anachronisms, the quaint traditions and tiresome rituals (some of which need to be changed as this ancient institution stumbles into the twenty-first century) I must say I am liking my new school. It is always fascinating, frequently exciting and, occasionally, you feel some of what you are doing may even be worthwhile. It is exhilarating, and challenging, to have the opportunity of beginning a new life here. On my desk I have a card sent to me by the Reverend Clifford Warren, Rector of Machen, a Welsh clergyman who, as I may have mentioned, was once in the habit of sending me telling maxims and homespun homilies so that I could share them with the viewing millions. On this card he has written: 'Beginning. The word "begin" is full of energy. The best way to get something done is to *begin*. It's truly amazing what tasks we can accomplish if only we begin. You're never finished if you for ever keep beginning.'

XYZ

Be ambitious.

Be brave.

Be courteous.

Be daring.

Be enthusiastic. ('Oh Lewis,' said Sybil Thorndike to her husband when they were both in their eighties, 'if only we could be the first actors to play on the moon.')

Be fair.

Be generous.

Be happy.

Be instinctive.

Be careful with jokes. (Remember: not everyone can recognise the difference between being light-hearted and being light-weight. You don't have to take yourself seriously in private, but in public it is advisable. Many people will rate you at the value you appear to place on yourself.)

Be kind.

Be lively (but don't over-do it).

Be mindful of others. (The American journalist David Halberstam formulated a rule for success in politics: 'Always stay in with the outs.')

Be nice. (Sometimes you may need to be nice and tough, but, as a rule, only the second-rate need to be nasty.)

Be optimistic.

Be prepared. (A supporter said to John Bright that a speech

'smelt of the lamp'. Bright replied, 'Young man, I have never heard a speech worth listening to that didn't.')

Be different.

Be restrained. (A colleague's account of Iain Macleod at Cabinet meetings: 'When he had a point to make he made it with brevity, relevance and force. If he had nothing new to contribute, he did not speak unless invited to do so.')

Be straightforward.

Be truthful.

Be unembarrassed. (When you do something embarrassing, once it's over, forget it. Everyone else has. Remember, apart from your parents, no one is interested in you, except yourself.)

Be vigorous. (Action this day!)

Be wise. ('A man should never be ashamed to own that he has been in the wrong, which is but saying, in other words, that he is wiser today than he was yesterday.' Jonathan Swift.)

Be *you* – and never mind X and Z. They're for Scrabble. This is for real. Enjoy!